KEIKO'S JOURNEY

Dear Jean,
Wishing you a life
filled with joy, friendships
and wise learning.
  Kay Hwang

Copyright 2015
By Kay Hirai
All rights reserved
ISBN 978-1-63405-000-5
First [1] edition
Printed in Canada by Imprimerie Gauvin
Cover art and book design by Dan D. Shafer
Typeset in Adobe Caslon, Montserrat, and Eureka Sans
Illustration of Shiro and author by Kay Hirai

Production assistance from:

CHIN MUSIC PRESS
1501 Pike Place #329
Seattle, WA 98101
www.chinmusicpress.com

KEIKO'S JOURNEY

A MEMOIR BY
KAY HIRAI

*This book is dedicated to the memory of my parents,
Mary Fujiye and Tatsunosuke Tadamatsu; my dog, Shiro;
and to all those in Japan and the United States
whose lives have been altered forever by the
devastating effects of World War II.*

TABLE OF CONTENTS

Foreword *1*

1. Siren 3
2. Egg 6
3. American Soldiers 13
4. Soup Line 16
5. Shiro 22
6. Homecoming 26
7. Abuse 30
8. Lie 36
9. In the Dark Cave 41
10. Smell of America 56
11. Sad Day 59
12. Passport 62
13. Farewell to Japan 65
14. Baachan's Story 68
15. Shopping Adventure 72
16. The Truth 75
17. Survivor 84

Epilogue *89*
Glossary *91*

FOREWORD

It was soon after I returned from my tearful trip to Kokura, Kyushu, in Japan that I finally felt comfortable in my own skin. As I stepped off the plane at the Seattle-Tacoma Airport, a definitive moment occurred when I said to myself, "Keiko, you are home. You belong here. Now, go forward and pursue your dreams."

For the first time in my life, I was able to free myself from the painful, yet nostalgic memories of growing up in Japan in the aftermath of World War II. I realized how selfish I would be if I didn't make the effort to share my story. Even though it is the recollection of many memories from past years, it is really a contemporary story that applies and is relevant to the millions of immigrants, migrants, and refugees, young and old—groups that live in two worlds, yet feel as though they don't belong in either one.

I was an only child of a second-generation Japanese woman, Fujiye. She was born and raised in the United States, but immigrated to Kokura in her early twenties. Her uncle, who was childless, adopted Fujiye as his daughter. She lived a seemingly hopeless life—a loveless marriage that was assigned by her uncle, inferior status of the Japanese female, and painful secrets that had to be kept from her daughter.

I was deeply impacted by my mother's experiences. As hurtful as many of those were, they are, and always will be, a part of me. I often wonder how I survived a childhood with only my dog, Shiro, to share my constant emotions of confusion and fear. I also wonder how these painful struggles eventually led to my self-discovery and my life's purpose.

The dates and timeframes that I have indicated in this book may not be totally accurate, but they reflect my best recollected memories between the ages of five to eleven.

I hope you enjoy my life story.

Kay Hirai
November 2015
Seattle, WA

CHAPTER 1:
SIREN
KOKURA, JAPAN, 1945

We stood on top of a hill, Mari and me. The sky was crystal clear, except for a few floating clouds that resembled thin sheets of white gauze. Yellow and black butterflies fluttered around me, eventually resting on the wild flowers that peeked out amongst the tall grass. The field of rolling, green grass stretched far into the distance, and I wondered where it ended.

My friend, Mari, who lived close by, was three years older than me. She was tall compared to other girls her age. Her long, thick, shiny, black hair was gathered into a rubber band and pulled to the back of her head. I didn't know why she paid attention to me, a girl so much younger. I enjoyed going to the bookstore with her, where we would spend hours looking at the books we wished we could buy. I looked up at her as though she was the older sister I didn't have.

It was a typical July afternoon in Kyushu, the southern island of Japan. The temperature was in the 80s. It was too hot for adults, but perfect for us children. On this day, my mother asked Mari if she could go with me to the fields nearby to pick some yomogi leaves. She needed them to make my favorite manju. I loved eating this special Japanese confection filled with azuki bean paste, neatly tucked inside the green covering made of rice flour and yomogi leaves. When eaten warm, it would melt in my mouth.

When we reached the top of the hill, Mari and I raced to pick the leaves.

"Keiko, this is a contest! Whoever fills her basket full of leaves will be the winner!" Mari exclaimed.

I proceeded to pick the leaves as fast as I could. In the end, Mari was the winner. After the race, we lay on the grass looking up at the bright blue sky, giggling and laughing as we picked and threw the wild flowers and grass at each other.

Mari said, "I can hardly wait to go home and help our mothers make the sweet manjus."

"Yes, we can have our own tea party!" I replied.

Suddenly, out of the clear blue sky, the shrieking sounds of the air raid sirens were around us. The loud, shrill sounds with short pauses seemed to come from all corners of the land. We stood paralyzed, staring into the sky as the siren grew louder and louder. I covered my ears with both hands and screamed, "Mari, Americans are coming to attack us!"

"Keiko, remember what our mothers told us?" Mari said, with a look of panic in her eyes. "Drop everything and start running for home. Quick, hold my hand and keep up with me!" Mari commanded. I started to cry, "Mari, I don't want to leave all the leaves." She screamed, "No, drop them and let's go!"

I ran as fast as I could, trying to hold onto Mari's hand with a tight grip. I stumbled and fell, and felt my body rolling down the hill, out of control. I heard Mari's panic stricken voice, "Keiko, stop!"

The sound of the siren kept coming, closer and louder.

Mari came running down the hill, slipping and sliding, but kept her balance.

"Keiko, get up," she said as she pulled me, grabbing my hands.

"Be strong and hurry," Mari said, looking terrified.

I ran as fast as I could with all my might. It seemed like forever.

When we finally stumbled into the familiar streets of our neighborhood, our mothers came running up to us.

"Keiko and Mari, you made it back!" Mother said with a sigh of relief.

There were screaming voices and people running in the streets as frantic mothers gathered up their children.

When we reached the front of our house, I saw two bags on the ground that mother had packed with food and clothing. Ojiichan, mother's elderly uncle, sat by the door, ready to leave.

"I will carry the large bag. You carry the small bag," Mother instructed me.

Mother strapped the canvas bags over her shoulders and mine. She stretched out her arm and told Ojiichan and me to hold on to her hands. "We must go now," Mother said. From the sound of her voice and the terrified look in her eyes, I knew I had to obey her every command. Hand in hand, we ran to the underground shelter.

When we reached the front of the tunnel leading to the shelter, I saw a mob of people shoving and fighting their way to get in.

"Ready?" Mother asked us. "Hold on tight and never let go!" Using the force of her 105-pound body, she pushed her way through the tunnel opening. I squeezed my eyes shut and hung on, feeling people's bodies pushing and shoving against me.

When I opened my eyes, we were inside a pitch-black cave.

Mother said, "Ojiichan and Keiko, we made it in. We are safe now. Are you both all right?" I let her know that I was fine, even though my body ached and my knees felt raw from the tumble I took on the hillside.

Mother turned on her small flashlight and examined me. It was then that she noticed my injury.

"Keiko, it looks like you had a bad fall. I will put some medicine on your knee," she said.

I could no longer hold back my tears and cried, *Okaachan* (Mom), it hurts!" Mother gently held me in her arms and rocked me as she wiped my tears away with her hands.

Mother looked at Ojiichan, who was huddled on the other side of her and asked, "Ojiichan, *omizu wa do desuka?*" (Would you like some water?)

He replied with a weak and raspy voice, *"Daijobu. Arigato."* (I am all right. Thank you.)

I looked at Ojiichan and saw that he looked weak and tired. I reached over and squeezed his hand and said, "Ojiichan, *oyasumi.*" (Good night, Uncle).

He nodded his head and tried to give me a smile.

Mother told us to get some rest. As I closed my eyes, I heard the moaning sounds of adults and children crying in the dark cave. I felt the sweaty bodies of people, pushing against me to find more space. I forced myself to keep my eyes shut and tried not to think about the throbbing pain in my knee.

I wondered where Mari was. The vision of us picking yomogi leaves on the green hill with the blue sky above gave me comfort in this darkness.

CHAPTER 2:
EGG

We had been in and out of the underground shelter for months. It was a hot and muggy August morning in our city of Kokura. The air was still. I could hardly breathe. "No sirens today," I mumbled to myself. It felt eerie.

My upper arms itched from boils. The skin around the infections was red and swollen. The boils were filled with white pus. Mother scolded me when I touched them.

"Keiko, leave them alone. If you pick at them, they will break open and cause more infection and then you will be one sick girl."

"Mother, I can't help it. They are bothering me!" I cried.

"Look, I have them all over my body, too." She pulled up her blouse to show me. Her upper body was covered with sores.

"You have more boils than me," I said, looking away.

"They will disappear when we get some nutritious food into our bodies," Mother said.

"I'm hungry. My stomach feels empty!" I cried, suddenly remembering how hungry I was.

"Keiko, hurry and get dressed. We will go to the store and get some food. Ojiichan is hungry, too," she said. "Tomorrow, if there are no sirens, we will take the train to Kurume. That is where Uncle Koji and Aunt Kame live. Your grandmother, who lives in America, told me that if we need rice, we can ask her younger brother, Koji. He owns a small rice field and would have ample rice to share with us.

I quickly got dressed. "Mother, I'm ready. Let's go to the store."

We walked eight blocks. The temperature was already climbing and we wore straw hats to protect us from the harsh rays of the sun.

We stepped into the small, shabby store. The dirt floor was hard and uneven. Wooden shelves with scattered cans of food lined both walls. In the center of the store were crates half-filled with mountain potatoes.

Mother pointed to the corner of the room, "Look Keiko, eggs!"

I ran to the box. There lay three brown eggs nestled in a pile of shaved wood.

"Mother, these are beautiful! I haven't had any in a long time!" My mouth watered.

Mother reached into the box. She took out two of the eggs and carefully wrapped them in newspaper. "You and Ojiichan can eat these raw — more nutritious that way."

"Why only two, Mother? We need three. One each for Ojiichan, you, and me," I said.

Mother quickly looked away and said, "No, we are getting only two."

"Why, Mother? Aren't you hungry, too?"

"Keiko, you heard me. Please don't argue." She then walked over to the box of mountain potatoes and placed three in her cloth bag.

Then I saw my favorite rice crackers in a shiny, cellophane bag on the shelf.

"Look, Mother, this is my favorite snack! May I get a bag?"

"No, Keiko, put it back."

"Why? I want them. I'm hungry and my stomach hurts," I wailed.

Mother stood firm and said, "No. I said put it back." She pulled the bag out of my hands and returned it to the shelf.

I cried incessantly all the way back to the house.

"I'm hungry! My stomach hurts!"

Mother walked in silence. She held my hand while carefully carrying the mountain potatoes and the two eggs that were nestled in the crumpled newspaper inside her burlap bag.

"Keiko, you must learn to *ga-man* (maintain self-control). We will be home soon."

Ojiichan lay in bed when we arrived home, too weak to get up.

"We are home!" I called out. I ran over to his bed and reached for his hand.

"Did you have a nice trip to the store? Were you a good girl?" he asked.

I nodded my head and said, "Guess what Mother bought for you? An egg! She said you should eat it raw."

Mother came in, holding a tray with a steaming cup of tea and a small bowl of rice. A raw egg with its orange-colored yolk sat on top.

"Ojiichan, please eat the rice and egg. This rare treat will help you gain strength."

Mother helped him to sit up. "Keiko, hold Ojiichan's back while I give him the food."

Ojiichan nodded and said, "Thank you, Fujiye, for your care. You are the best daughter I could have. I thank my sister for sending you from America."

He slowly ate the food that Mother fed him from the bowl. For a short while, as I watched Ojiichan eat, I forgot about my own hunger.

Vivid memories of Ojiichan and me spending time at the park flashed through my head. It seemed only a few months ago that he was young and healthy.

I remember his robe was a neatly pressed Japanese hakama. The dark wooden *geta* (sandals made of wood) showed off the white of the *tabi* (white socks with divisions between the toes). With his graying mustache and shiny bald head, Ojiichan looked like a distinguished professor.

"Keiko, let's sit down on this bench for a while and enjoy the scenery," I remember him saying. We watched the birds as their heads bobbed up and down, picking up seeds from the ground. The neatly raked gravel in contrast to the lush green leaves of the cherry trees made me calm and peaceful.

Ojiichan started to sing a Japanese children's song in a soft voice. "Suzume no Gakkou no sensei wa…muchi o furi-furi chi pa-pa." I joined in singing this song about little sparrows being taught by their teacher who swung a wooden stick as she chirped.

After enjoying a lunch of rice balls, sweet and sour plums, and fish prepared by Mother, we left the park. I hated to leave. Spending time with Ojiichan was my favorite thing to do.

Mother and I sat down to eat our meal after Ojiichan went back to sleep. She served me the raw egg, sliced mountain potatoes, and hot tea.

"Don't eat so fast, Keiko. This is all you'll have to eat today," said Mother.

I ate slowly and enjoyed every bite of my dinner.

Mother ate her sliced mountain potato and pickled radishes.

"Keiko, go to bed early tonight. Tomorrow, we will take a train ride to Kurume. Remember? Uncle Koji and Aunt Kame own a rice field and they will give us some rice."

The next morning, Mother and I boarded the train at Kokura station and headed south. After two hours, we arrived in Kurume. When I stepped off the train, I noticed that the scenery was different. Farmlands planted neatly with rows of gold and green crops seemed to stretch for miles.

"Mother, what are they growing here?" I asked.

"Mainly rice, Keiko…steamed white rice that fills our stomachs come from these fields."

I couldn't take my eyes off the wide-open space.

"Keiko, let's hurry. We have to walk to Uncle Koji and Aunt Kame's house now," Mother said. She looked at the address on a small piece of paper. "We are very close, let's hurry!"

I walked fast to keep up with her.

Uncle Koji's house, made of dark, brown wood, was big. His yard was clean and neat. Hens roamed along the side of the house, constantly clucking. As their heads bobbed up and down, they picked up little seeds from the ground.

"Mother, I've never seen hens in anyone's yard. Why are they here?" I asked.

"They lay eggs. Uncle Koji and Aunt Kame can enjoy eating them," Mother said.

"You mean they can have eggs every day?"

"Yes, they also have chicken meat to eat when the hens get older."

"They can't do that to the chickens! They are cute and alive just like us," I said feeling sorry for them.

Mother nudged me softly, "Shh-h-h. We are almost to their front door. They might hear you."

Uncle Koji and Aunt Kame greeted us at the door. "Fujiye and Keiko, it's so nice of you to come for a visit. It's been a while!" said Uncle Koji.

He had thick, grey hair and a round, happy face and looked more like a businessman than a farmer. The traditional black hakama he wore looked crisp and perfectly fit his stocky body.

Aunt Kame chimed in, "Oh my, this is Keiko-chan? She's so grown up. We remember when she was a toddler."

Aunt Kame had a small face with dark skin. Her graying hair was pulled back tight in a bun. The kimono she wore had a navy and white design, typical of those worn by older Japanese women.

"Please come in. You must be hungry. We have some tea and sweets for you," said Aunt Kame, leading us into their guest room.

Sliding shoji doors covered the front of their house. As I entered the room, I gasped at the beauty just beyond the windows. There was a clear view of the expansive greenery that surrounded the house.

We sat on the tatami mat around a low, wood table where the food was served.

"Tell me Fujiye, how is my older sister doing in America?" Uncle Koji asked. "Has the war affected her as much as it has Japan?"

"My mother wrote to me a while ago. The last I heard, Americans had imprisoned them in an internment camp with barbed wire all around. I have not heard anything since. I think about them constantly and pray for their well-being," Mother replied.

"I miss my older sister. I don't know why she and her husband went to live in such a far-away land," Uncle Koji said, shaking his head.

"Mother often told me that she wishes to return to Japan one day."

"Fujiye, how is my older brother doing in Kokura?" Uncle Koji asked.

"Thank you for asking. Ojiichan's condition has been declining. The war has taken a toll on his health."

"He is fortunate that you are there by his side. I know you are taking good care of him. Fujiye, I want to thank you for that."

"Ojiichan sends his regards," Mother bowed politely.

The tea served was hot and soothing to my stomach. The manju, made of flour and filled with sweet chestnuts, made me smile with pleasure. After I ate one, I stopped. I remembered what Mother told me during our train ride. "Keiko, when manju are offered, don't take more than one. You don't want Uncle Koji and Aunt Kame to think you are greedy."

Uncle Koji pointed at the dish of manju and said, "Keiko, please eat another one."

"No thank you, Uncle Koji. I'm full now," I managed to say, even though I was dying to have another sweet manju.

"What brings you to Kurume?" asked Uncle Koji.

"Mother told me when Keiko and I need food, go to Kurume and ask Uncle Koji for help. She said you will give us rice."

"Oh, I see. Perhaps we can give you some rice to take home," said Uncle Koji.

Aunt Kame gave him a piercing look with her eyes. She leaned her body forward and looked Mother squarely in the eye. "Fujiye, I know you are having a difficult time. With the war devastating Japan, we are all in the same boat. The rice we grow on our farm needs to provide for our two married sons and their children. We have three families to feed. I wish we were in a position to help, but the truth is, we can't."

I saw the disappointment on Mother's face. Her eyes welled up with tears, but she quickly wiped them away and said, "Thank you, Uncle Koji and Aunt Kame. I understand that you are struggling, too."

Mother got up and said, "Keiko, we must go. Our train will be arriving shortly to take us back to Kokura. We must hurry."

Mother faced Uncle Koji and Aunt Kame and bowed her head. "Thank you for letting us visit. I am happy to see that you are doing fine." She gave me a nudge to do the same.

"Uncle Koji and Aunt Kame, thank you for serving me the sweet manju. I liked it very much," I said with a polite bow.

"Fujiye and Keiko, try to come and visit again. We will be praying for my sister's safety in America," said Uncle Koji as he opened the front door to let us out.

We walked briskly to the station and boarded the train going to Kokura. Mother sat in silence, looking out the window all the way home.

Sadly, Ojiichan passed away the next day. His body was bathed by the neighboring men. Mother dressed him in a dark-colored hakama. His white mustache was trimmed. His body lay in our house for three days. During this time, many people came, chanted, and rang bells while sitting beside his body. On the fourth day, he was given a ceremony by the Buddhist priest and sent off to heaven, which was appropriate for a respected man in Kokura.

Mother held my hand as we sat listening to the priest chanting. She whispered in my ear, "Keiko, Ojiichan will be happy now. No more struggles of the war…he will have plenty of food to eat in heaven."

"Will Ojiichan be singing chi-chi-pa-pa, chi-pa-pa in heaven?"

"Yes, he will still sing to you."

"Will Ojiichan have enough eggs to eat?"

"He will have more eggs than he could possibly eat."

The next day, America dropped the atomic bomb on the nearby city of Nagasaki. The city was destroyed and thousands of people died. We heard on the radio that Japan's emperor accepted defeat and declared America's victory.

CHAPTER 3:
AMERICAN SOLDIERS

I have no memory of when the war ended. When did the sirens stop? When did we stop running into the dark cave? It seemed like it happened quickly, almost overnight.

Suddenly, I saw hundreds of men dressed in American military uniforms walking around our streets. They strolled in groups of twos and threes. Some soldiers had light skin, sandy-colored hair, and blue eyes. Others had darker faces with tightly-coiled black hair that was cut close to their heads.

The soldiers with darker faces intrigued me. They had huge eyes and their faces were shiny. When they smiled, their mouths expanded into wide grins, showing large, white teeth that filled their mouths.

All the soldiers had several things in common. They were tall and their uniforms were pressed to a smooth finish, with sharp creases in their trousers. They also had well-trimmed haircuts and nails.

The soldiers were friendly to us. When I passed them on the street with my neighborhood friends, Mari, Hideki, and Yoshiko, they stopped and gave each of us a stick of chewing gum. After we said our polite "thank you," they patted us on the head and said, "It is nice to meet you. Are you being good children?"

We bowed our heads to show them our respect.

I was puzzled as to why the American soldiers were in our city. I asked Mother all the questions I had swirling around in my head. "Who are these men and why are they here? Why do they look so different?"

Mother sat me down and looked at me intently as she said, "You are too young to understand, but you should know that our country lost the war.

America dropped two atomic bombs on our major cities, Hiroshima and Nagasaki. Japan had no choice but to surrender. I'm happy that America won. But, at the same time, I am sad that Japan lost. Those soldiers you see on our streets are United States servicemen. Unlike Japan, America is made up of many races. This is the reason why there are soldiers with different skin colors."

Mother continued, "These soldiers were sent to Japan to help us recover from the aftermath of the war. You should not be scared of them. They are here to help us. America has already begun sending aid to our schools and food banks. You will see that getting rice will become easier for us."

Shortly after our talk, Mother began working at the American army base in Kokura. She became a secretary and translator for an American officer named Colonel Roberts.

On her first day of work, as she prepared to leave, she said, "Keiko, what do you think?" I turned and was immediately surprised to see that she wasn't wearing her usual drab-colored kimono. Instead, she wore a brightly-colored sweater that matched a tweed skirt, with western-style, high-heeled shoes in brown. Her hair had waves and curls. She even moved differently than when she wore a kimono. She stood taller and took longer steps as she walked.

"Wow, Mother. You look just like the pictures of American women I've seen in the magazines!" I said enthusiastically.

After school, I often visited Mother at work. I was amazed to meet her Japanese co-workers. They were men and women who were just like her. They talked with each other in English and I could see Mother felt comfortable and enjoyed this work environment, complete with American Coca-Cola drinks, pencils, and tablets.

One day, when I went to visit Mother at the Army base, she introduced me to her boss, Colonel Roberts. He invited Mother and me to come into his office for a visit. He was a tall man with sandy colored hair. His neatly pressed uniform was decorated with medals and badges. His office walls were lined with framed photos and awards. The tall bookcase on one side of his office was tightly packed with black binders and books. I whispered to Mother, "He must be a very important man."

"Colonel, I'd like you to meet Keiko. She came by to say hello after school," Mother said.

"*Keiko, doudesuka?* (How are you doing?) Mary has told me a lot about you. She told me that you are a bright student in school and also the same age as my own daughter."

"My mother's name is Fujiye, not Mary," I corrected the Colonel.

Mother stepped in and said, "Keiko, don't worry. Mary is my American name, so everyone calls me by that name here at work."

It was the first time I heard that my Mother's name was Mary, and I felt left out because I didn't know.

Our lives changed after Mother started working at the army base. People who had previously been friendly began taunting her, saying, "Traitor, go back to America." When this happened, she would tell me, "Just ignore them—they think I am siding with the Americans. In their eyes, I am considered a traitor. Keiko, for your own good, never tell anyone that your Mother is an American citizen or that she works for the American military."

I made my promise to her saying, "I will never tell anyone."

CHAPTER 4:
SOUP LINE

The northern winds whipped through my second-grade classroom at the Hiagari Shougakkou Grade school in Kokura. The broken windows in our classroom rattled and shook as the winds kicked up. Cardboard and newspapers that were nailed to the window frames were ripped away with each gust of wind. Pieces of torn newspaper lashed around the room like a whirlpool. We ducked our heads to avoid being hit by the flying paper.

"Children, quickly line up and walk to the entrance of the school," said Kimura sensei. We marched to the main entrance of the school.

Two men stood on each side of the entryway with containers of the chemical DDT strapped to their backs. Their gray uniforms completely covered them from neck to toe. Their masks covered most of their face. Kimura sensei stood by their side. She bowed and said, "Thank you, gentlemen, for volunteering your time to help eradicate our school's lice epidemic."

"Hurry students, stay in line and move quickly. We need all your heads sprayed before class begins," Kimura sensei said, as she gently gave some students a push to keep the line moving towards the men.

It was my turn to get sprayed. "Step up close to me, close your eyes tight, and hold your breath," the man said. I heard a loud hiss of air. The ice-cold spray hit my scalp. Then came the lethal powder stinging my nostrils and eyes. Tears rolled down my face. Trying not to breathe, I clenched my fists and stood still.

We looked like dust mops as we returned to our classroom.

Kimura sensei greeted us with a smile. Her long hair was neatly tied back and fastened with a wide, black ribbon. "Good morning students. Thank you for tolerating the DDT. I know this is not easy for you, but it's necessary to stop the growing lice problem in our school. The war has ended, but life is still difficult. Let's be thankful and concentrate on our studies. I know you are strong and will get through this."

We bowed, and in unison shouted, "Good morning, Kimura sensei. We will have a good day!"

My classmates and I sat in our seats, bundled up in layers of clothing to keep ourselves warm. Most students wore clothing that was too big, worn out, or often with holes scattered throughout the material. I felt lucky to have my pink and grey, argyle sweater and a brown, wool jacket that my grandmother in America sent to me.

"Students, get your books out. We will be starting the kanji class. Do you remember our lesson from yesterday?" She unwrapped a small piece of chalk from her carefully folded handkerchief and began writing the characters on the blackboard for the words HOUSE, SKY, SUN, TREE. Even with her careful touch, the chalk crumbled and dusty pieces fell to the floor.

Sitting in this drab classroom, lined with long rows of wooden-slab tables and stools, it was difficult to concentrate on what was being taught. I sat shivering, with only one thing on my mind—lunch time. I wanted hot soup so my body would warm up.

I sat next to my best friend, Yoshiko, who lived two blocks from me. She lived in a house with a fence, enclosed by a large wooden gate. Inside, well-shaped bonsai trees lined both sides of the gravel walkway.

Yoshiko's father owned the Kometani Department Store, a prestigious retailer in downtown Kokura. The Kometanis were one of the few wealthy families in our area.

Mr. Kometani came home late in the evenings, arriving to hot meals prepared by Mrs. Kometani. He was a tall man and wore custom-made, dark suits befitting his title as president of the Kometani Department Store.

When he saw us doing our homework on the dining table, he said, "I'm glad to see that you girls are studying hard. Studying is the only thing you should be doing. Your middle-school entrance exam will be coming in a few years."

I enjoyed spending evenings at Yoshiko's house when her two older sisters, Mika and Aya, were home. Mika, the older sister, had long hair that was neatly braided. Her pale skin and slender face flattered her quiet and intelligent manner. Aya was the exact opposite of her older sister. Her cheeks were blushed with color, resembling a shiny apple on each side of her face. She made me feel at home when I visited by giving me a warm welcoming hug. Mika and Aya often played *Karuta* (a Japanese card game) with us. We laughed and giggled, watching each other flip the colorful cards, trying to get the perfect match.

I wished Yoshiko's two sisters were mine.

At Yoshiko's house, there was enough food for everyone. Her mother made sure that everyone left the table with full stomachs. She often made us bowls of noodles. The tasty broth, made of seaweed and dried fish flakes, slid quickly down my throat, warming my body. I loved hearing her happy voice say, "Girls, I have more noodles and broth. Don't hold back, eat until you're full."

I wondered how she could stay so trim when she cooked so much food for her family.

There were over 20 students in our second-grade class. Most of the students played together, except for a lone group of four students; these students lived on the other side of the railroad tracks. They came to school in shabby clothes, full of holes. Their shoes were old and beaten, barely covering their feet. Their bodies smelled like outhouses.

Masao, the leader of this group, was a tall, stocky boy with hair chopped in clumpy, uneven pieces. His skin was purple and his body looked bloated - like he had been drinking too much water. The seat of his pants was torn and the skin of his buttock exposed a large boil that was swollen.

One day after school, Yoshiko and I were walking home, chatting about the school day. Suddenly, Hideki, the boy who lived next door to me, came running behind us. He was one year ahead of us in school, but seemed younger. He lived up to his nick name, *Kozo* (a trouble maker), by pulling pranks on the neighborhood kids every chance he got.

"Keiko and Yoshiko, wait for me," Hideki screamed. When he caught up, he had an impish grin on his face. "Hey, do you girls want to go on an adventure?"

"To where, Hideki?" I asked.

He pointed toward the railroad tracks and said, "Across there."

Yoshiko and I looked at each other and shook our heads.

"Keiko and Yoshiko, come with me. Let's go see where Masao and his friends live. Our mothers won't know," Hideki coaxed.

I remembered Mother saying, "Keiko, don't you ever go across the railroad tracks. That's where the *kojiki* (street bums) live. You will be sorry if you get lost in that area because no one will be able to find you."

"Come on Keiko and Yoshiko. Let's go pay Masao and his friends a visit," Hideki persisted.

I looked at Yoshiko and said, "Should we go with him?"

She shrugged her shoulders and said, "I'll go as long as we keep this a secret from our mothers."

"Okay, it's a deal. Let's go," said Hideki, as he motioned us to follow him.

When we crossed the tracks, we immediately saw rows of small shacks made of worn, wooden boards tacked together with rusty nails. There were no windows or doors. Through the open spaces in front, anyone who was passing by got a view of the lumpy dirt floor and the shabby, makeshift furniture in the interior of the shacks.

We came upon a shack that had piles of broken chairs and metal pilings in the yard. A few green leaves peeked out from an old wash tub filled with dirt on the side of the shack.

"I think this is where Masao lives," Hideki whispered.

We peered into the dark shack. There was a dug-out area with a pile of burnt coal in the center of the room. A large cooking pot, supported by a makeshift frame, hung on top. I was shocked to see the how badly Masao lived. I had never seen anything like this.

Suddenly, we saw Masao come out of the house.

"What are you guys doing here? You don't belong here. Go back to your own neighborhood!" As he yelled, he shook the rock he held in his hand as though he was going to throw it at us.

Hideki held up his hands and begged, "Masao, don't throw it. We didn't mean any harm. We just wanted to find out where you lived."

"Why, so you can make fun of me?" he hissed. "Get out of here!"

"Let's go, Keiko and Yoshiko," Hideki said.

We quickly crossed the tracks and ran home as fast as we could.

A week later, at school, it was finally lunch time. Kimura sensei announced, "It's Keiko and Yoshiko's turn to get lunch and serve it to all of us." We walked down the hallway to the kitchen. There was a six-woman lunch crew in this room, all wearing white aprons. Their mouths were covered with masks made of white gauze. They stirred the hot soup in silence.

The smell of food made our mouths water. One of the women gave us a large bucket of steaming broth with rice and a sprinkling of vegetables. "Here you go. Make sure to dole it out carefully so that every student gets a full bowl." Yoshiko and I bowed and said, *"Arigato, Obasan."* (Thanks, older woman).

The soup bucket was heavy. Yoshiko and I walked the entire length of the long hallway, balancing the bucket between us.

When we entered our classroom, the students were already lined up, ready to receive their soup. The students who sat in the front rows were the first ones in line. Masao and his friends stood at the end. I poured the soup very carefully for each student, making sure there would be enough for Masao and his friends to have a full serving. After I poured a generous portion of soup in Masao's bowl, he walked back to his seat, being careful not to spill any of his lunch.

Masao drank his soup with a vengeance. All of a sudden, he started to choke and cough, spurting the soup out of his mouth. His stomach started heaving and his body doubled over. A few seconds later, he threw up everything on top of his desk. I ran over to him and was horrified at what I saw. A large, white worm wriggled and slithered in the yellowish liquid that he had vomited. I screamed, "Oh no, Masao, what is happening? Kimura sensei, please help Masao!"

She quickly came over and ordered everyone, "Please keep calm and go back to your seats. I will take care of this."

Masao was quickly guided out of the classroom and did not return for the remaining hours of school.

I had a difficult time going to sleep that night. I lay awake, huddled under my soft futon covering. I closed my eyes tightly. I tried to fall asleep, but all I could see was Masao's pale face, shamed and disgraced as he watched the white worm that came out of his body.

That night, I dreamt that hundreds of giant, white worms were chasing Masao and me. We were running as fast as we could, but they were catching up to us. "Masao, I can't run anymore. I will get eaten up. Someone help us!"

I heard Kimura sensei's voice from far away, "Keiko and Masao, come back to class. Our kanji class is starting!"

I screamed, "Kimura sensei, we can't! The worms are right behind us and they are going to eat us alive!" One giant worm caught up with Masao and slithered up his leg. Masao screamed, "Get off me, bastard, or I will stomp you to death!"

The worm hissed, "We both have to survive — it's you or me!"

I felt someone shaking my body. When I opened my eyes, I saw Mother's face. "Keiko, wake up, you were having a bad nightmare. You were gasping and screaming. Tell me what's wrong."

"Everything, Mother. Everything." I flung the covers over my head and turned toward the wall.

CHAPTER 5:
SHIRO

My second grade homework was more difficult than usual. I sat on the tatami mat in my house, intent on learning a new group of kanji words. I stared at the large, mandarin orange and two pieces of rice candy wrapped in bright cellophane. They were just beyond my reach. Mother had left them, saying, "Only after you finish your homework."

The loud barking of a dog broke the silence of this quiet afternoon in September. I ran to our front door to see what the noise was about. Mother stood at the entry, talking to a tall American soldier with sandy-colored hair. A pint-sized, white dog stood obediently by his feet.

"Keiko, this is Jim," said Mother. I stood by Mother and looked up at the tall American. His soldier's uniform was neatly pressed. I couldn't take my eyes off of the sharp crease lines on both of his trouser pant legs.

"How are you, Keiko?" Jim said with a big smile on his face.

I bowed politely and replied, "Kon-nichi-wa."

"Keiko, this is my dog, Shiro," he said as he bent down and stroked the dog's head.

"Can you say hello to Keiko?" Jim said as he looked down at his dog.

Shiro instantly responded with a few barks that sounded like a mixture of barking and whimpering. She jumped up and licked my hand. I pulled my hand away quickly and wiped the wetness off on my skirt.

"Don't worry. Shiro won't hurt you. She is very friendly and she loves children."

"Keiko, Jim works with me at the American army base. Jim has received orders to return home. He asked if we would adopt Shiro and give her a safe home," Mother said.

"What?" I asked in a puzzled voice.

"I told him you are an only child and might like having a friend. Jim and Shiro are very close and he is looking for someone who will love her as much as he does. I told him you are very kind to animals. What do you think?"

I looked at the pint-sized dog that stood by Jim's feet. She was pure white except for a small black tip on her right ear. Her body was thin, as though she had been running for miles every day. Her dark, brown eyes were shaped like almonds. She had a wet, black nose that looked like a round button. She was the cutest dog I had ever seen.

Jim said, "Shiro will make a nice pet if you can teach her to mind you. But, I have to warn you. She is strong-willed and a little difficult to handle at times. But, once you gain her trust, she will become your loyal friend. Go ahead and pet her head."

I walked up to Shiro. I bent down and put my hand on her head. She looked at me with her dark almond eyes. The moment Shiro and I looked into each other's eyes, I knew I wanted her as my friend. "I want to keep Shiro. I will take good care of her and we will become best friends."

"Oh, I am so relieved that Shiro has found a nice family to live with," said Jim. He picked up the dog and snuggled his face into hers, as she licked his face profusely in return.

"Goodbye, pal. I will miss you. I will think of you in America. Be a good girl for Keiko and become her friend, okay?" Jim's eyes were moist. He quickly turned and walked away. Shiro followed him. I ran after Shiro and picked her up in my arms. I walked back to the front door as Shiro struggled to break free.

I took Shiro inside my house and talked to her gently. "I know you miss Jim, but I promise I will be your new friend." Shiro looked at me with the saddest eyes I had ever seen. Whimpering, she ran to the front door and scratched the glass. She walked back and forth across the doorway trying to find an opening to the outside.

For the next two days, I spent every free moment with Shiro, trying to get her to like me. I played fetch with a ball, tossed her bean bags on our tatami mat, and raced with her to get them. At night, I cuddled with her under my blanket. I was happy that she seemed to enjoy our time together. I loved how she would come running and jump into my arms and lick my face—just like I saw her doing with Jim.

Two days after Jim left, Shiro ran away. I felt discouraged and rejected. I asked Mari, Hideki, and Yoshiko to help me look for her. We went up and down every nearby alley calling, "Shiro. Come home!"

Shiro was nowhere to be seen.

"It's getting dark. I have to go home for dinner now," said Hideki.

"No…please don't go. Not until we find Shiro," I begged.

Suddenly, I saw a bolt of something white running across the street into a narrow walkway.

"Shiro, come back!" I said, using my loudest voice.

I ran as fast as I could to the spot where I saw her.

"I have rice candy for you. Come here!" I held the candy between my fingers and waved my hand back and forth in desperation.

Shiro came running from the alleyway. I slowly squatted and held out the rice candy toward her. I stayed very still and said nothing for fear of scaring her. She came toward me with a curious look on her face. I inched a little closer to her, showing her the candy in my hand. She came running to me and snatched the candy. I quickly put the leash around her neck and praised her by saying, "Good dog, now let's go home!"

Hideki, Mari, Yoshiko, Shiro, and I walked back to our neighborhood singing *Yuyake koyake-de-hi-ga kurete…yama no otera no kane ga na ru* (The mountain temple's bell rings in the light of a beautiful sunset)."

Jim was right. Shiro was a strong-willed dog who broke all the rules to get what she wanted. Shiro was determined to find her American soldier. A week later, she ran away again. I feared I would not find her. The thought of losing her was unbearable.

"Shiro doesn't like me. She must hate me to keep running away like this," I wailed and sobbed.

"Keiko, don't blame yourself. She likes you, but she just can't forget Jim. Stop crying and start looking for Shiro," Mother scolded.

I ran out of the house and went down the steps leading to the street. I saw a flash of white and then I saw her running up the street toward me.

"Shiro, you came back…you came back to me!" I screamed in delight. We had the best reunion as she jumped into my arms and licked my face until it was all wet.

For the next few months, Shiro and I were constant companions. I petted and praised her for every little thing she did. Mother bought me a book on how to train dogs and I taught her many of the tricks that were in the book.

"Shiro, you are the smartest dog I know." Each time she learned a new trick, I rewarded her with a small piece of rice cracker. She eagerly lapped it up, as though this was the last piece of food that she would ever eat.

Our friendship grew stronger. Instead of constantly running away, Shiro was at my side every moment of the day, except when I was in school. On most evenings after dinner, she followed me on a wild venture of catching fire flies in the dark. On weekends, she came with me to jump rope at the neighborhood lot or walked with me to a nearby pond to catch tadpoles with my friends.

One day she came to school and waited outside the gate. I was so happy to see her that I ran up and gave her a big hug. "Shiro, what are you doing here?" She responded by barking, jumping, and running circles around me. I took her action to say, "I couldn't wait to see you so I came to meet you!"

At that moment, I felt certain that Shiro loved me as much as I loved her.

CHAPTER 6:
HOMECOMING

Laughter and chatter from the students filled every hallway and classroom of the Hiagari Shougakkou. It was 3:00 p.m., our daily clean-up time.

"Whee, I'm going faster than you!" Hideki said to Goro, who was also in the third grade. They were on their hands and knees, pushing wet rags down the hallway.

"Wanna bet? I'm faster!" replied Goro, as he picked up speed.

Kimura sensei stood at the end of the hallway. "Make sure all the corners are wiped free of dirt."

"Look at me sensei. I'm fast!" said Hideki.

"I want to see more work and less chatter from you," she replied, using her scolding voice.

Kimura sensei motioned for Yoshiko and me to follow her to the classroom.

"Yoshiko and Keiko, your job today is to wipe off all the desktops, clean the windows, and sweep the floors."

"Come on Yoshiko, let's go to the closet and get the rags and disinfectant," I said. Yoshiko followed me to the storage area where all the cleaning supplies were kept. Two other students came and we cleaned each area that Mrs. Kimura asked us to.

"Ouch, I cut my finger on the broken glass!" said Yoshiko as she cleaned the corner of the shattered window.

"I hope the broken glass will get replaced soon. It is dangerous. It looks like just a small cut. I will clean it out for you," Kimura sensei said as she went to get her first-aid kit. She quickly wrapped a tape over Yoshiko's index finger and gave her a hug.

The final dismissal bell rang loud and clear. We all exclaimed, "Yippee, school's out! Thank you for teaching us, sensei! See you tomorrow!"

As I walked out to the playground, I heard the faint sound of Shiro barking by the gate. I looked into the distance and saw Mother and Shiro.

My dog looked like a white fur ball as she jumped up and down in her excitement to see me. "Shiro, come!" I commanded her in my happy voice. She dashed toward me with her tail spinning like a propeller. She jumped into my open arms and gave my face her usual welcoming licks.

"What are you and Shiro doing here?" I asked Mother.

"I took the afternoon off from work," Mother replied. "I thought it would be nice to walk to the park and spend some time with you."

"That sounds like fun. Let's go!"

The three of us walked leisurely to the park on our way home. We entered the gateway and walked to the bench where I had spent many hours with Ojiichan.

"Let's sit down, Keiko," Mother said as she motioned me to sit next to her. Shiro sat down on the ground between us.

Mother's face became serious. She took my hand and held it very tightly. "Keiko, I have something to tell you."

"What, Mother?" I said, looking closely into her eyes.

"I just received a notice in the mail that your father, Zenichi, is coming home from the war."

Not knowing what to think or how to reply, I sat in silence.

"Keiko, did you hear me? I said your father is coming home."

"Who is Zenichi, Mother? You never told me about him," I asked in disbelief.

"He is your father. I don't blame you for not remembering him. You were only two years old when he was drafted into the Japanese army. The last I heard, he was captured as a prisoner of war in Manchuria," Mother said. Her voice was shaky and low.

"Mother, why didn't you tell me about my father? You never said a word about Zenichi to me!" I started to cry, feeling angry and deceived.

"Keiko, I am as shocked as you are. I believed all these years that he was dead. I never heard a word from him. He was sent off to Manchuria to fight for our emperor. When Japan surrendered the war to the United States, Manchuria was invaded by the Russians. I heard all the soldiers were captured as prisoners of war at that time. I never dreamed he would make it out alive. I believed what everyone said: Soldiers who are captured and sent to the prison camps go through such harsh treatment that they rarely make it out alive."

"When will he be coming home?"

"The letter said he will be home in five days. Keiko, we must do everything we can to make Zenichi feel welcome. Please call him *Otouchan* (Daddy) when you first meet him. That will make him very happy," pleaded Mother.

I promised Mother that I would call him Otouchan.

The morning of my father's arrival, Mother made sure I wore my best going-out dress. I was surprised to see that she wore her Japanese kimono in subdued colors instead of the usual Western outfits that I had become accustomed to seeing her wear.

"Mother, why are you wearing your kimono instead of a sweater and a skirt?" I asked.

"Zenichi is not used to seeing me in Western clothes. I don't want to offend him."

Without another word, we hurriedly left the house to catch the bus to the train station.

The air at the Kokura-Machii train station was filled with excitement as families and friends of returning soldiers were gathered to welcome them home. Hundreds of small Japanese flags with red circles on white backgrounds waved in unison as the families sang the Japanese anthem.

"We've been waiting for a long time. When will the train get here?" I asked.

"Keiko, be patient and don't complain. Just think about all that your father had to endure in the war. You should be grateful that he is alive and coming home."

We heard the whistle to let us know that there was a train coming in.

"Oh, that must be the train with the soldiers!" Mother exclaimed.

The crowd around us screamed and chanted with delight.

The black train rolled in and came to a screeching halt. It seemed like forever until the doors opened. One by one, men dressed in mustard-green, Japanese army uniforms stepped off the train. The crowd was eagerly pushing and shoving, trying to reach their loved ones. Mother looked anxiously as each soldier stepped down.

"Zenichi, Zenichi! Keiko and I are here!" Mother shouted, waving her hands as she saw her husband stepping off the train into the station.

A soldier stoically walked towards us. He was short and thin, had a rough complexion, and thick, black wavy hair.

Mother gave me a sudden push. "Keiko, this is your father. Give Zenichi a big welcome home!"

"Otou-chan, welcome home!" I rushed up to him with open arms and threw myself into his arms.

"Keiko, is this really you? You've grown so big!" he exclaimed.

Mother stood behind me and politely bowed to her husband. Father walked up and gave her a long embrace.

"Fujiye, I'm sorry you had to go through the hardship of the war by yourself. But I can tell you did a fine job raising Keiko," Father said, as he wiped away the tears from Mother's face.

"I thought about you and prayed to *Kamisama* (God) that you would be alive."

"Tell me Fujiye, how is Ojiisan?"

"Zenichi, I'm sorry to tell you that he passed away shortly before the atomic bomb was dropped on Nagasaki," Mother said.

"He was a strong man, but the war must have taken a toll on him. I'm sorry to hear that," Father said.

"How about you? It's a miracle that you survived the harsh treatment in the prison camps of Manchuria," Mother asked.

"The only thing that kept me going during those dark days was the thought of seeing you and Keiko again," Father said as he stroked my head.

We stood together, hand in hand, and sang the Japanese anthem as it played over the loudspeaker.

After a few moments of silence, Father said, "Keiko and Fujiye, no more worries. I'm here to take care of you. Let's go home." Father's face was beaming with happiness.

On the way home, Father stopped at the liquor store in downtown Kokura. Mother and I watched him buy bottles of sake and beer to take home.

CHAPTER 7:
ABUSE

Morning glories lined the streets of our neighborhood. Every morning, white trumpet-like petals opened to their full glory as if to say, "Enjoy the coolness of the morning because the heat will surely follow."

Even though I had school projects every day, I loved summer vacations. I wrote in my diary, drew landscape pictures, composed haiku, and calculated math problems every morning. After I finished my school work, I went with the neighborhood kids to catch dragon flies and scoop tiny tadpoles in the small pond nearby. Mari and I rode our bikes to our favorite spot on the hilltop and picked yomogi leaves like we used to before the war.

One morning, Shiro sat patiently by my side as I worked on my math assignment from school. The minute I finished, I patted Shiro on her head and said, "I'm done. Let's set up our store!"

Her ears perked up. "Arf," she barked, meaning, "I'm ready!"

We ran to the backyard. I found three wooden crates that lay against the side of the house. I dragged them to the front entryway and turned them upside down to create counter tops. Then, Shiro and I ran into the house. I slid open the closet door and picked up the stack of boxes containing my treasures. One by one, I carefully brought them outside and unpacked each box, arranging the treasures on top of the crates. Bottles of colored water, gold-foiled candy wrappers, and *ohajiki* disks (glass marbles) of many colors. My highest-priced item were the *otedama* (small hand sewn fabric bags filled with beans) that Mother had helped me make. I spent many hours perfecting my juggling act by tossing these colorful balls in the air and catching them as they came down.

I rang the cowbell and shouted, "Keiko's store is now open!"

Hideki, Yoshiko, Mari, and other children from the neighborhood came running, each clutching a wad of play money.

Shiro jumped and turned in circles to display her excitement.

"You've been working hard, Keiko. Look at all the nice things you've made!" exclaimed Mari.

Hideki asked, "What's inside these bottles?"

"They are different-flavored soda waters. Try the green one. It tastes like lime."

"How much?" asked Hideki.

"Only five cents."

"I'll take it."

He lifted the bottle to his mouth and pretended to drink it.

"Yikes. This tastes strange. I want my money back!"

"Don't give him his money back, Keiko. He drank it already," said Yoshiko in her typical motherly way.

"I'll never shop here again." Hideki puffed up his chest and pretended to walk away.

Other kids bought candy wrappers, otedama balls, and ohajiki disks with the fake money. Mari and Yoshiko played with the otedama balls, throwing them high into the air and catching them. When one of them dropped the ball, they giggled and tried to be the first one to pick it up so that they could claim it as their own. Some kids played the game of ohajiki, using the glass disks. They spread a handful on the ground and snapped them with their fingers, trying to create a collision of disks.

We were having fun, not paying any attention to the setting sun.

"Keiko, your father is coming up the stairs. It must be late," said Mari.

Father, wearing his dark suit and a tie, walked toward me.

"Well, what do we have here? Can I buy something, too?" He leaned over to hug me. At that moment, I smelled the stink of sake on his breath.

Suddenly, I didn't feel like playing anymore. I felt queasy in the bottom of my stomach.

Father pinched my cheek in a playful way and walked into the house.

"Mari and Yoshiko, I want to close the store now," I said.

"Don't you want us to help you put your store away?" asked Mari.

"No, I can do it myself. Please go."

"We're not done having fun yet. Come on Keiko, let's keep playing," whined Hideki.

"You heard Keiko. The store is closed," Mari said as she walked the neighborhood children to the street.

Mari and Yoshiko stayed with me for a while, but knowing there was nothing they could do to help my sudden mood swing, they left.

I began to put my store away. Shiro watched in silence.

I had put the last ohajiki disk away when I heard the roar of the jeep coming up our street. The sound from the erratic sputtering of the engine jolted our quiet neighborhood. I ran down to the end of the block and saw Mother sitting in the front seat next to Colonel Roberts.

"Mother, Shiro and I came to meet you. Let's walk home, please."

"What's wrong Keiko?"

"I smell alcohol on Father's breath. When he hears the sound of the jeep coming up our street, he gets angry."

"Is something wrong, Mary?" asked the colonel, not understanding our rapid Japanese.

"No, nothing," Mother replied. "Thank you very much for the ride. I'd like to walk the rest of the way with my daughter."

Mother got out of the jeep and we walked up the street to our house.

When we reached home, Father was standing in front of the house. Colonel Roberts roared past us in his jeep.

Muttering, Father went inside the house and Mother followed him.

My body shook. I wanted to jump out of my skin. Huddled at the base of the closed shoji screen with Shiro sitting close to me, we heard Father's angry voice grow louder.

Shiro whimpered.

"Shhh, Shiro. Be quiet or we'll get in trouble." She cowered and licked my face over and over in an attempt to comfort me.

"Why does your boss give you a ride home?" Father yelled. "You're trying to sneak behind my back, aren't you?"

"I am doing nothing wrong, Zenichi. Colonel Roberts is happily married with a wife and daughter. He lives up the hill, so he asked if I wanted a ride," Mother replied.

"You don't think I notice how different you act when you're around your friends at the army base? Laughing and flirting. You never act like that in front of me."

"Americans have a different way of socializing than we Japanese do."

"Oh, so you're saying being Japanese isn't good enough?"

"No, I never said that."

"You're no better than a whore! You think I'm stupid because I don't speak English. I know what's going on. You're flirting with them."

"Please stop this nonsense. Nothing is going on. The alcohol is making you crazy."

"Well, I'll show you how whores get treated!"

I heard the yelling of Father's voice and a cry from my mother, followed by the sound of her body hitting the wall.

"What should I do, Shiro? I wish I had enough courage to walk in and tell Father to STOP!"

I jumped up and ran out of the house. I didn't know where to go. I went down the street toward Yoshiko's house. Shiro followed me, barking loudly. I reached her front gate and ran up the walkway. I pounded on the door.

When Mrs. Kometani opened the door, she looked startled.

"What's wrong, Keiko?" she asked.

"Come to my house and stop Father from hitting Mother. Please, come now!"

"Keiko, I can't go with you. I don't want to interfere with your family's affairs. I'm sorry," she said, quickly looking away from me.

"If you don't come, he'll kill her!" I sobbed.

"I am sorry, but I can't help." She softly closed the door, leaving me standing alone.

Dejected, Shiro and I went back home. The house was silent except for the sound of Mother sobbing.

Father greeted me with a smile. "Keiko, where did you go?"

"I went to Mrs. Kometani's house," I answered.

"Why?"

"I didn't want Mother to die. I went to ask for help."

"Don't you ever do that again. Everything is all right now, so don't worry."

I stood there, not knowing what to say. I felt confused. Father walked out of the room.

Shiro gazed at me with her innocent brown eyes. "Shiro, you are the only one I can trust. I'm so glad I have you." I picked her up and held her close. Her warm body gave me assurance and made me feel safe — for now.

A few minutes later, Father came out from the back room carrying his summer jacket.

"Keiko, remember I told you we're going to the parade? Tanabata festivities begin at six o'clock. We'd better hurry!" he said in his happy voice.

"How about Mother? Will she be coming with us?" I asked.

"She won't be coming. Just you and me."
Not knowing what to say, I left the house with him.

The annual Tanabata Festival took place in downtown Kokura on July 7. It is said that Princess Orihime and Prince Hikoboshi, who were heavenly lovers, were separated by her father, Tentei, who was the Lord of the Universe. The Tanabata festival commemorates their reunion once a year when the Milky Way opens up and the couple is reunited.

Father and I approached the town center. The air was filled with the smell of grilled food. The strong, pounding rhythms from the taiko drums made my heart jump with excitement. Colorful flags adorned both sides of the street. Men and women dressed in blue and white summer *yukata* (village kimono made of cotton) lined the center of the street, waiting for the procession to begin.

"Look Keiko, those floats are big, aren't they?" Father said. "When you grow up, you can ride on one, too."

"Really? I can hardly wait!" I tried to be excited, even though my heart felt heavy.

"Let's go where the vendors are."

Rows and rows of vendors were lined up along the parade route. Each booth had a canvas roof. Storefronts were lined with displays of colorful trinkets, candies, and children's toys.

"These stores are just like mine!"

"Keiko, I will buy you anything you want tonight."

I looked through all the trinkets and squealed in delight. I picked out a doll dressed in a red Japanese kimono. "She is so cute!"

"Give it to the lady, Keiko. I will buy this doll for you."

"Ureshi!" (I'm so happy!)

"Look here, a larger doll. Do you want this one, too?" Father asked.

"I only want the little one," I replied, feeling guilty that I was not accepting everything he offered to buy for me. I wondered how he could be so nice to me when a few hours ago, he was a raging maniac towards my mother.

"Come on, pick another doll. I want to buy you more." He looked at me with a coy smile.

I knew that Father was trying to be cheerful and generous to make me forget the scene that occurred only two hours ago. I felt guilty that I was caught up in the excitement of the festival while Mother sat alone at home.

Two weeks later, we celebrated Obon, where the spirits of our ancestors visit their families. Father did not drink during the three days of this holy holiday. I was happy that Ojiichan's presence in our house kept Father sober.

"Keiko, Ojiichan is here visiting us for three days. If you listen very carefully, you might hear him singing to you," Mother said.

I went to the park where Ojiichan and I had spent time together. I sat on the same bench where we used to sit and closed my eyes. Mother was right. I heard his voice singing my favorite sparrow song, "Chi-chi-pa-pa chi-pa-pa. Suzume no gakkou no sensei wa, muchi o furi-furi, chi-pappa."

For a few minutes, I felt his gentle presence next to me.

There were many Obon ceremonies that took place during this time. Mother dressed me in a summer yukata made of bright-colored cotton and I danced the traditional Bon Odori in the park after sundown. Hundreds of lanterns were lit, giving the dark night a feeling of warmth.

At the end of the third day, we made a little straw boat with a candle secured in the center. We took it to the river and placed it in the water. I watched as Ojiichan's boat floated down the river with others. It looked as though hundreds of flickering candle lights were floating in the darkness of the night. Shiro ran on the side of the river, barking.

"Say your farewell to Ojiichan, Keiko. He loved you so."

"Goodbye Ojiichan. I love you," I said as his boat floated down the river.

"He is going back to heaven now. He will be back to visit us again next year."

I made a silent promise to Ojiichan that Shiro and I would look after Mother.

We walked home in the warm summer night.

Shiro jumped up and down, reaching to catch the light from the swaying lantern that Mother held.

CHAPTER 8:
LIE

Our yearly train ride from Kokura to the city of Fukuoka was crowded. Passengers pushed and shoved trying to find seats. The stale air made us weary and fatigued. I sat on Mother's lap for the two-hour ride. Mother had ordered me to give up my seat to an elderly woman who was standing because no one had offered her a place to sit.

"Keiko, hold your belongings very tightly. There are many pickpockets on this train."

"Are they bad people?" I asked.

"No. The war has left them with nothing and they are desperate."

I clutched my bag and hoped no one would steal it.

The train pulled into Fukuoka station and came to a screeching halt. A cluster of people stood on the platform, waving small red and white Japanese flags. "Keiko, welcome!"

"Look Mother. They've come to get me!"

"Do you remember Fukuoka no Obaachan, Uncle Torao, and all your cousins?"

"Yes, I remember them from last summer!"

In the center stood Obaachan and her son whom I called, Uncle Torao. He was unusually tall with a kind face. A delicate and attractive looking woman who stood next to Uncle Torao was Aunt Fumi. She wore a simple white kimono with a blue obi. The three adults were surrounded by the children, Sumako, Kiyoko, Chiyoko, and Tomo. Mother told me they were my cousins but I didn't know how they were related to me.

"We've been waiting for you to arrive!" called out Sumako, the oldest cousin.

Obaachan stepped forward and hugged me as though she would never let me go. "Keiko, you've grown taller. I've been dreaming about you for a whole year!" Her dark kimono gave out a faint scent of wisteria flowers.

Obaachan looked at Mother and said, "Fujiye, thank you for bringing

Keiko to us. She will have a good time with her cousins for the next two weeks."

Mother bowed her head low to show respect to Obaachan. "Thank you for inviting Keiko to spend time with you and her cousins. She has been counting the days, looking forward to seeing all of you."

After a few minutes of awkward silence, Obaachan looked at me.

"Keiko, say goodbye to your Mother. She will be going back to Kokura on the next train."

Mother gave me a hug as she whispered in my ear, "Be a good girl. Mind Uncle Torao and Obaachan. Your father will be coming after you in two weeks to bring you back to Kokura."

I watched Mother as she walked toward the station where a northbound train would be arriving to take her back to Kokura.

"Mother, please take care of Shiro until I get back home!" I called out.

She briefly turned around and nodded. I felt the urge to run after her. I hated the thought of her going home alone. I hoped that Father would stay in a good mood while I was gone.

Mother's image quickly faded, swallowed up by the mob of people who were rushing to catch their train to Kokura.

"Keiko, let's go home," Obaachan said as she held her hand out to take mine.

After walking through many streets lined with houses and small stores, we finally reached the home where Obaachan and Uncle Torao lived. The large, two-story house looked like the ancient houses I had seen in the samurai movies. As we entered its *genkan* (entryway), I took off my shoes and lined them up, facing outward toward the street. Mother had told me this was the proper way to enter someone's house when you are a guest. I walked up two steps and entered the main living area.

The room was sparse and the floor was covered with tatami mats made of straw. I recognized the large photo of a handsome, young man who was dressed in a white navy uniform. His white-gloved hands rested on top of a sword that stood erect between his knees. He looked straight ahead. His face was stern and strong.

Obaachan stood beneath the photo and bowed.

"Tatsunosuke, my beloved son, Keiko is here to visit with us. Hasn't she grown tall?"

She prompted me to do the same. I bowed to the man in the photo.

"Tatsunosuke is happy to see you Keiko. Did you see him smile as you entered the room?"

"Yes, Obaachan, he smiled at me," I replied, even though I was only trying to be agreeable.

For the next two weeks, I was busy with my life in Fukuoka. Uncle Torao and Obaachan took my cousins and me to the park, to downtown Fukuoka's stores, and to visit other relatives who lived nearby. My cousins and I played every spare moment we had. We jumped rope, watched the outdoor puppet shows, and bought *tako-yaki* (grilled octopus) from the street vendors.

My favorite time of the day was when Aunt Fumi taught me to play the piano. She was very gentle and kind. She taught music in a grade school in Fukuoka. I learned the piano keys quickly due to her patience and encouraging words.

One afternoon toward the end of my stay, Obaachan said, "Keiko, let's you and I have some quiet time alone."

"Now Obaachan? Sumako and Kiyoko are waiting for me outside. We are going to jump rope."

"Keiko, you will be leaving us in two days. Let's sit down under Tatsunosuke's photo. You can play later."

I reluctantly obeyed and sat down with Obaachan on a cushion under the photo.

She placed a burning incense stick and a bell on a small wooden box. She sat down, carefully folding the edge of her kimono underneath her legs. *Ojuzu* (Buddhist prayer beads) beads were draped on her hands as she bowed her head and prayed silently. After a minute, she hit the bell softly with a wooden dowel.

"Tatsunosuke was my youngest son. He was bright and a most honorable young man. He lived up to the samurai name he was given and he has never disappointed me." Her eyes welled with tears. "War does cruel things to parents. Tatsunosuke was called to fight for his country in the Japanese Navy. He was only thirty when he died in the jungles of the Philippine Islands. He was too young to die."

"Obaachan, what did Tatsunosuke do before he went to war?"

"He was a fine detective who worked for the police department."

"Did he get married?"

"Yes, he was married. He left behind a wife and a baby girl."

"Obaachan, what happened to his wife and baby girl?" I asked.

Breaking the mood of the moment, voices came from the entryway. "Keiko, are you coming to play? We are waiting for you!"

I jumped up. "Obaachan, Sumako and Kiyoko are calling me. They're waiting for me to come out and play. May I go?"

"Keiko, don't be disrespectful to Tatsunoske. "Obaachan's stern voice startled me.

I challenged her. "I've heard the story of Tatsunoske many times Obaachan. Can you tell me again later after I get back from playing jump rope?"

"Keiko! Do you know who this man is?" Obaachan stood and towered over me.

I quickly sat down.

She looked down at me with piercing eyes. I saw the hem of her kimono quivering. I immediately knew that I had deeply insulted her.

"Yes, he was your son," I said nearly whispering.

"Look at me, granddaughter!"

I raised my trembling eyes. Obaachan was pointing to the photo.

"Keiko, Tatsunoske was more than my son. He was YOUR FATHER!" Her voice was hoarse and crackled as she yelled.

"That's a lie!" I leaped to my feet. "I already have a father!"

I ran out of the house, past my cousins who were still holding their jump ropes, open-mouthed with astonishment.

"It's a lie, it's a lie!" I screamed as I ran up the street.

Obaachan and I did not bring the subject up for the remainder of my stay in Fukuoka.

On the day I was to leave, I waited by the entryway with my suit case packed. When I saw Father walking toward the house, I ran up the street to meet him and fell into his open arms.

"Otouchan, I thought you'd never come!" I exclaimed.

By the time we walked back to Obaachan's house, the whole family was gathered in the entryway.

"Thank you so much for having Keiko spend the time with you. As usual, I am sure she enjoyed her stay." Father bowed his head respectfully towards Obaachan.

She stepped forward and gave me a long hug. "I will be waiting until you come to visit us again next year." She had tears in her eyes as she waved farewell.

"Keiko, we have two hours before the train to Kokura arrives. Let's go to the park and go for a boat ride." Father said.

"Ureshi," I replied.

At the park, Father rented a little red boat and rowed it to the middle of the small man-made lake. When he stopped rowing, he opened a small paper bag and showed me the rice crackers and milk candy that were inside.

"Here you go. I brought your favorite snacks for you," he offered a handful to me.

"No, thank you, Father. I'm not hungry."

"Keiko, this is not like you. Is something wrong?" he asked.

I looked away from him and said nothing.

"What's wrong Keiko? I can tell that something is bothering you. Tell me," he said.

"Obaachan told me that her son, Tatsunosuke who died in the war, is my father. I called her a liar."

"Is that what she told you?" Father asked with a worried look on his face.

"Yes. She told me when we were sitting under Tatsunosuke's photo that hung on her wall."

"She must be getting feeble. Of course you shouldn't believe her. She was telling you a lie. How could you have another father? I am your father."

I reached across and hugged him. "I'm so glad! I wouldn't know what to do with two fathers!"

After the boat ride, we rode the train back to Kokura chatting and laughing all the way.

CHAPTER 9:
IN THE DARK CAVE

Nothing could have prepared me for what turned out to be one of the most frightening days of my life. It was a bright, sunny day in mid-July. When I woke up, I was anticipating that I would have to tackle every activity on that day's schedule: exercise in the morning, help clean up the neighborhood in the afternoon, and do my homework in the evening. Even though we were on a break, the school assignments continued. There were the daily journals, scenery paintings, and collections of butterflies and bugs that had to be kept up throughout the summer.

At breakfast, Mother sat next to me. She sipped a cup of tea and watched me as I delightfully ate a raw egg cracked over a bowl of hot, steaming rice. "Keiko, how fast you've grown. You are already finishing up the third grade. Remember those days when you cried, begging me to buy you a fresh egg? We should be so thankful that those days of constantly being hungry are over."

"Yes," I replied, thinking about the infected boils on our bodies at that time. My face cringed as I pictured the itchy, throbbing sores in my mind again.

Mother abruptly ended our conversation, got up, grabbed her purse, and called out, "Aki-chan, please come in here so that I can give you instructions for the day, before I leave for work."

Aki-chan was a girl Mother had hired for the summer to watch over me and the house. Aki-chan was from the countryside. Her frizzy, black hair, which was pulled back tightly with a rubber band, made her look more old and plump than she really was. She wore a white, cotton blouse and a black skirt every day. Her hands were always red and swollen, something that I wondered about. Despite her plain and unattractive appearance, I found her to be gentle, kind, and fair. She would scold me when I was wrong, but would treat Shiro, my dog, with respect and endearment every time she saw her.

When Aki-chan entered the room, she immediately sat down on

the tatami-mat, neatly tucked her knees underneath, and bowed her head politely.

"Aki-chan, please remember all the activities that Keiko has to do today. Don't forget that there is laundry that needs to be washed and hung outside to dry. Lastly, Zenichi will be arriving home from work at 5:00 p.m. Make sure that his cold beer and snacks are set out for him." For some reason, Mother spoke in an unusually strong and direct tone of voice as she gave these instructions.

"Hai, wakarimashita" (yes, I understand), replied Aki-chan with her head still lowered.

As Mother started walking toward the front entry, Aki-chan stood up, ran to the sliding door, and opened it for her. She bowed and said, "Don't worry Ma'am, you can trust me to do all the things you asked. And Keiko-chan will stay safe. Have a nice day."

I ran up the stairs to my house, exhausted and famished from the rigorous exercise program and neighborhood clean-up. *"Tadaima!"* (I'm home), I shouted as I entered the open doorway.

Aki-chan came running from inside the house and said, *"Irashai* (welcome home), Keiko-chan. Shiro-chan and I've been waiting for you. I made cold soba noodles, knowing you'd be hot and hungry when you arrived home."

"Thank you, Aki-chan. That sounds good!" I walked into the room and immediately smelled the fish sauce that had been poured over a big bowl of noodles decoratively topped with sliced *kamaboko* (fish cake).

Aki-chan and I sat down and slurped down the noodles. We even had a contest to see who could slurp the loudest. Aki-chan roared with laughter as she watched me exaggerate the motion of sucking the noodles. Shiro whimpered beside us, wanting to join in on the fun. Aki-chan went to the kitchen and returned with a small bowl of noodles for Shiro. She quickly ate it and glanced at Aki-chan, her eyes begging for more.

Aki-chan scolded her saying, "Shiro-chan, no more."

We both laughed as Shiro continued to beg, raising her paw as though to shake our hand, and then, rolling over-and-over trying to please both of us.

Keiko dressed up in a New Year's kimono.

TOP: Kokura no Ojiichan
MIDDLE: Fujiye and Keiko
BOTTOM: Tatsunosuke Tadamatsu

FACING PAGE, TOP: Colonel Roberts
FACING PAGE, BOTTOM: Tatsunosuke in his naval uniform.

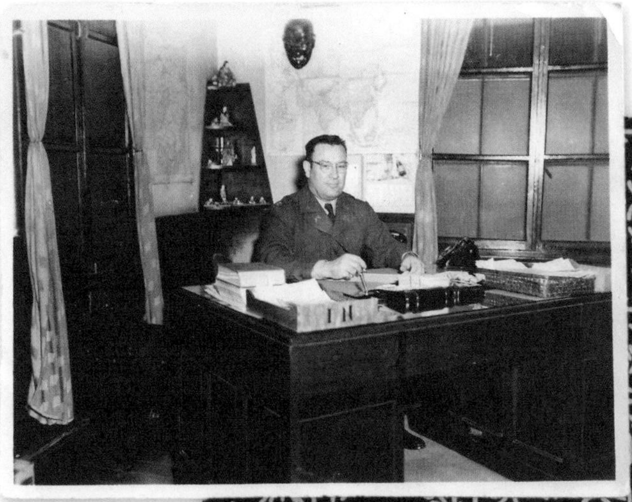

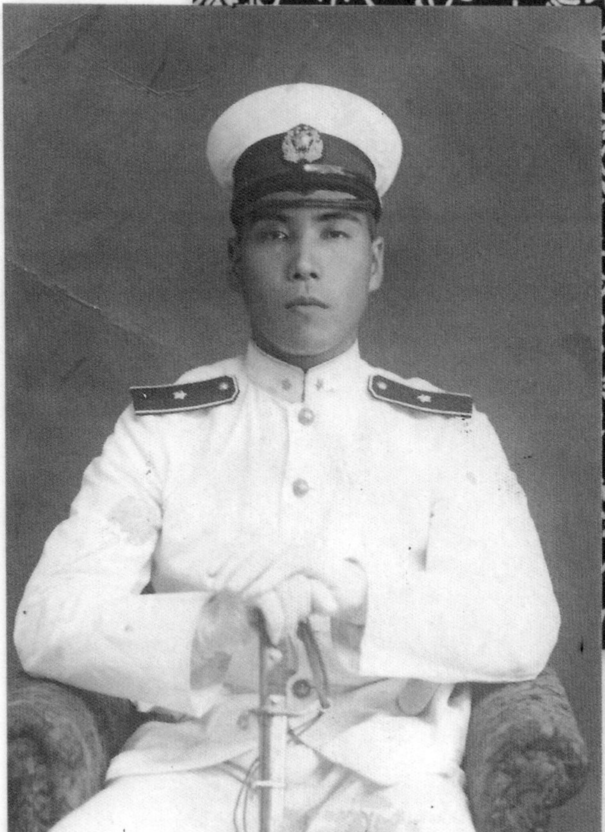

Fujiye, Keiko and Aki-chan

TOP LEFT: Fujiye and Tatsunosuke on their wedding day.
TOP RIGHT: Keiko at three months.
BOTTOM: Hiking with school friends.

Tatsunosuke, Keiko and Fujiye.

TOP: Keiko and Fujiye at the school's undoukai day.
BOTTOM: Keiko and Fujiye in Seattle.

TOP LEFT: Keiko with her father, Zenichi, and mother, Fujiye.
TOP RIGHT: Keiko, Yoshiko and a neighborhood friend.
BOTTOM: A school play.

Aki-chan said, "Keiko-chan, you must be tired, why don't you take a short nap? I will be busy washing clothes in the yard, but call if you need me."

"I will lay out my homework and will be ready to begin immediately after I get up," I said.

"That's a good idea," responded Aki-chan.

I opened the closet, got the box labeled "SUMMER VACATION HOMEWORK" and lifted the top. Inside was a wooden case with a sliding glass cover that displayed a variety of different insects. Step-by-step instructions pasted on the back of the case explained how to catch and treat live creatures using formaldehyde, so insects could be kept permanently displayed in the collection. The thought of killing living things made my stomach turn. I looked at Aki-chan with pleading eyes. "Can you please do this for me? Come with me into the forest so we can catch the insects together."

"I can't. Your mother asked me to spend the afternoon doing the laundry. Keiko, don't worry about it now. You are getting cranky. Once you get some rest, you will feel differently." Aki-chan left, closing the door behind her.

"No, I won't! I hate killing beautiful butterflies!" I wailed, rolled over and covered my head with a futon.

~~~

I was awakened by Shiro's wet tongue licking my face. I whispered, "Shiro, do you want to go into the woods with me? We can find the butterflies and insects ourselves." Shiro's ears perked up and her tail began to swing back and forth.

The house was quiet. I knew Aki-chan was doing the laundry, so I carefully got out the wooden insect cage and net. Then, I put on my canvas shoes and snuck out.

Shiro and I walked for what seemed miles before we entered the wooded area, a place where the air was cool from the shade of the bamboo trees that lined both sides of the trail. Shiro ran and frolicked between the bushy underground.

I yelled, "Shiro, come and stay close to me or you will get lost. Now help me look for some bugs that may be crawling on the ground."

Suddenly, three boys jumped out of nowhere. Each had a stick in his hand.

The boy in the center said to the others, "There she is. That's Ezaki Keiko, our enemy. Our fathers are dead because her mother ratted on the Japanese military. Isn't that so, Keiko?"

I was frightened and couldn't stop shaking. I stood there speechless. Shiro sensed the danger and began to growl. The boys wore dark clothing that made them look like ninjas. They scared me.

"We see your mother and you riding home in American jeeps. You think you're better than us because you get all those privileges from the Americans."

I whispered, casting my eyes down and shaking my head, *"iie"* (no).

"Why don't you go back to America and take your mother with you? We don't want people like you living in Japan," he said as he lunged toward me, holding a stick over his head as though he were going to strike me. I stepped back with a gasp, covering my head with both hands. Shiro suddenly advanced forward with a fierce bark. The boy kicked Shiro with his foot and she rolled over, making a shrieking noise that pierced my ears.

I screamed, "Don't hurt my dog!"

"Your dog is American, too. We know you got it from an American GI. We should kick it until it dies!"

I quickly picked up Shiro and started running away. I headed toward an underground cave where Mother, Ojiichan, and I were often evacuated to during the war to escape the American planes that were flying over us.

The boys walked at a slow pace behind me, all the while chanting and shouting, "Go back to America, traitor!"

Once inside the cave, I leaned against the wall of the cave, totally out of breath. It was dark, cold, and scary. I couldn't see anything, but I could still hear the voices of the boys outside threatening, "Don't come out because we will kill your dog if you do!"

My arms felt so numb I thought I would drop Shiro. I finally slid down the cave wall and sat on the ground, still hanging on to her whimpering body. I felt a trickle of something wet running down Shiro's thigh and knew it was blood from the wound the boy had inflicted on her. "Shiro, please don't die. I'll protect you, so don't worry," I said softly kissing her sweet face in an attempt to calm her.

As I sat in the darkness with Shiro, the surroundings became very still and silent. I wondered if the boys had left or if they were still waiting for me to come out. I had no way of knowing. Sitting there trapped, I couldn't help but think that this was my *bachi* (punishment). I had disobeyed my parents; they had warned me of the dangers of being alone in the woods. When I snuck out of the house, I had betrayed Aki-chan. Even worse, my innocent Shiro had been hurt. I felt terrible. Tears ran down my cheeks as I sobbed. I knew I would have to hide out in this dark cave for a while, but I did not know for how long.

When I heard footsteps coming from the back of the cave, I started to tremble. Shiro began to bark and I screamed. A shabby-looking man suddenly appeared and held a faintly lit lantern in his hand. He had a greyish-colored beard and wore a tattered shirt and baggy pants. The straw *zori* (thongs) on his feet looked as though they would break apart with a slight tug.

"Don't worry, I won't hurt you. What brings you here little girl?" he asked with a raspy voice.

"Bad boys came in the woods and hurt my dog," I said, sobbing.

"Let me see your dog. I can put some ointment on his cut to stop the bleeding," he said, as he came closer to examine Shiro's wound. You're lucky they didn't kick her in the stomach. That would have been the end of your dog."

He shuffled slowly toward the back of the cave. Searching amongst bundles of paper and blankets, he came back with a small tube in his hand. He knelt close to Shiro and reached for her leg.

Shiro squirmed and tried to get away from the man. I felt a sense of panic, but from his gentle demeanor, I sensed that I could trust him.

"Keep still, Shiro. This man will help you," I pleaded.

When she calmed down, the man put some of the salve on his forefinger and dabbed it onto Shiro's thigh.

"She'll be all right now. This ointment will keep the infection from spreading to her leg," he said.

"Thank you," I said.

The man nodded his head and said, "You are welcome."

"Why do you live in this cave? Are you homeless?" I asked.

"I have no one left in my life to go home to," he said with a shameful look on his face.

"Where are your wife and children?" I asked.

"I came home from the war alive, but my family was gone. They had been killed by the bombs that were dropped on our city by the Americans. I couldn't believe it. If anyone should have died, it should have been me." His eyes moistened as he continued, "So, what do I have to live for? I'm satisfied living as a hermit in this cave. I see no one and no one sees me."

I didn't know what to say. I felt sorry for the man. I wished Kamisama would bring his family back. I wanted to comfort him, but I didn't know what to say.

The man walked further into the cave, toward his belongings, and sat down on a pile of blankets. He said, "The war has a way of changing our lives. One day, you are surrounded by your loved ones, and the next day, you are alone in this world to live a lonely life. Poof, they are gone just like that."

I sat there intently listening to this man talking about the hardship he had gone through fighting for the Japanese army.

Suddenly, my heart jumped. I could hear my Otouchan's voice calling me, "Keiko, where are you? Please answer me!"

As I rose to leave, the man said, "Promise me little girl, don't tell anybody about me living in this cave. Do you understand?"

"Kojiki-san, I won't tell anyone," I promised.

I ran to the front of the cave holding Shiro tightly in my arms and yelled out, "Otouchan, I'm coming!"

I saw him standing by the trail and ran into his open arms.

"Keiko, what were you doing in the cave? Your mother and I have been worried sick over your whereabouts. Do you know how long you've been gone? Aki-chan said she last saw you in the early afternoon."

I tried to tell him the terrifying things that happened to me and Shiro, but a flood of tears suddenly came running down my cheeks. All I could get out of my mouth were a bunch of mumbled words that didn't make any sense.

I walked home with Otouchan as he carried Shiro in his arms. I was eventually able to tell him what had happened to Shiro and me.

When we arrived home, Mother came rushing over to us wailing, "Zenichi, thank you for finding Keiko. Is she all right?"

"Mother, I'm so happy to be home," I told her as she embraced me.

Mother pushed me away, looked sternly into my eyes and said, "Keiko, don't ever do that again."

"Where is Aki-chan? I need to tell her that I'm sorry," I said, peering around the house.

Father said, "Keiko, she is gone. We had to let her go."

"No!" It was not her fault. I did a bad thing. Please go and bring her back," I pleaded.

"Your mother and I will not change our minds," Father said.

I cried and stomped my feet as I told them, "I'm the bad person. Please don't blame Aki-chan for what I did."

As Mother hugged and calmed me down, she said softly, "Don't be so hard on yourself. It's been a long and terrifying afternoon. Shiro was hurt, but she will always love you. As for Aki-chan, she has been returned to her family, but she learned a valuable lesson and will be better prepared in the future. Now, please come and eat your dinner."

Mother proved to be right about Shiro. The next morning, she was jumping excitedly and was affectionately licking my face again. The guilt I felt about Aki-chan, however, remained unchanged. I missed her terribly. I also felt overwhelming sadness for the homeless man who was so kind to Shiro and me. I kept my promise and never told anyone about him. My daily prayer for him was that he would be able to eventually leave the cave and find happiness.

I don't understand why we have wars. Peoples' lives are changed forever.

I will never forget the things I experienced on that dark and frightening day.

CHAPTER 10:
THE SMELL OF AMERICA

On a snowy December afternoon, the air inside the house was so chilly that my nose was cold to the touch. I was bundled in layers of sweaters and heavy wool pants made by Mother. I sat in the *kotatsu* (a low table and quilt with a heater underneath). Because it was so cozy, Shiro instinctively pressed up against me as if she couldn't get close enough to my body. Obviously content, she spent hours huddled under the blanket and napped while I read my favorite Japanese books.

Mother called from the entryway, "Keiko, come quickly. A huge box arrived from your Baachan in America. Help me carry it!" I immediately ran to help Mother. Shiro jumped up quickly and followed. The cardboard box sitting in the doorway was made of corrugated cardboard and covered with tape everywhere imaginable. It had been tossed and dragged so much that the edges of the box were on the verge of splitting open.

I helped Mother pull the box into the house and place it by the kotatsu. Shiro circled the box, sniffing every inch of it and not knowing how to interpret the strange smell. Mother brought over a kitchen knife.

"Keiko, keep Shiro away from the box. This knife is very sharp and I don't want her to get hurt." I quickly reached for Shiro and held her tightly in my arms as she struggled to get loose, wanting to see what was in the box with the interesting smell.

"Shiro, hold still!" I scolded her as she whined and whimpered.

Mother cut the rope. Then, she punctured the tape and slid the knife along the seam of the box. I helped by pulling open the top lid. All of a sudden, a strange smell filled the room. Unlike the scent of Japan that was woodsy and clean, the aroma that came from the box was warm and sweet.

"Uum…Oooh… I love this smell!" I exclaimed. I was overcome with the excitement of what exotic treasures might be waiting for me. I put my hands deep inside the magical box and started to scoop out the items.

"Keiko, calm down. Take your time and carefully take out one thing at a time, starting from the top."

Shiro jumped on top of the box and looked in. As she admired the contents, she eagerly dug her face deeper into the box, detecting a smell which enticed her. Finding what she wanted, her teeth immediately gripped a cellophane bag filled with dog biscuits. Proud of her accomplishment, she jumped off the box and ran to the corner of the room to guard her newly-found treats.

"She is so lucky. Baachan remembered to put in a bag of treats for her, too," Mother laughed as she saw Shiro ripping open her present from America.

The box was filled with treasures that I had never seen—a dozen, individually-packaged pieces of chewing gum, Dagwood and Katie Keen comic books, and iron-on embroidery kits.

As I searched again, I came across a large box tied with a pink ribbon. "Oh-h-h…What's in this big box," I wondered.

"Open it and see," Mother said with a twinkle in her eyes.

I carefully removed the ribbon, opened the lid and gasped. Inside was an almost life-sized baby doll with huge eyes and a porcelain face.

"Keiko, take the doll out of the box. Baachan was excited for you to have it!"

As I lifted the doll out of the box, her blue eyes with long eyelashes made a clicking sound and blinked at me!

"Mother, did you see that? Her eyes opened and closed!"

"That's not all. Feed her some water from the baby bottle in the box," directed Mother.

I quickly ran to the sink and filled the small bottle with water. I put the nipple in her mouth and watched the water disappear.

"Now, check her diaper, it will be all wet," Mother said.

Mother was right. I felt the diaper and it was damp.

"Now, turn her upside down and give her a light tap. She may want to burp."

I faced the doll down on my lap and gave her a light patting. The doll cried, "Mama, Mama!"

When I did it again in front of Shiro, and the doll cried "Mama, Mama," she jumped and ran away, looking scared.

"You will have to get used to her voice, Shiro. This talking doll is your friend, too," I said laughing.

This baby doll, with her winking eyes, became my second best friend—a perfect gift for someone who longed for a sister.

Finally, the box was empty. Shiro and I sniffed the scent lingering in the box.

"This is what America must smell like!"

CHAPTER 11:
SAD DAYS

The sun seemed brighter than usual. I was feeling good from the high test score I received in my fourth grade class.

"Keiko, you are learning your kanji writing well. I have no doubt that you will pass your upcoming exam." Kimura sensei's words were encouraging.

"Thank you Kimura sensei. I will continue to study hard," I said, bowing my head respectfully.

"Don't let up on your homework. There will be another test coming next week," said Kimura sensei.

"I won't, sensei!" I said as I cheerfully ran towards the front gate of the school.

Walking home, I thought about the warm pudding Mother often made for me, my favorite after-school snack. In anticipation, I walked more quickly up the hill to my house. Shiro came running down the street to meet me. She ran circles around me as if to say, "I'm so happy to see you!" I gave her a hug, saying, "Shiro, were you a good girl today?" Shiro happily licked at my cheeks. We walked the short distance to our house and climbed the stairs to the front door.

I opened the sliding door, calling, "I'm home, Mommy!"

The house was silent. As I walked toward the back room, I could see Mother kneeling on the tatami mat with her head down sobbing. Her huddled body was shaking like a leaf.

I got a sick feeling in my stomach. The tightness in my chest made me feel as though I would instantly suffocate. I bent down, picked up Shiro, and held her close to calm me.

Nervously, I questioned her, "What's wrong, mother? Where is Father? Has he been drinking again? Did he hurt you?"

"No Keiko, it's not that," she replied sadly. "I received terrible news from America. My older sister, Annie, died giving birth. I keep thinking that this can't be true." Mother began to sob uncontrollably. "We were very close. I don't know how I will be able to go on," she said trying to hold back her tears.

"Mother, don't cry. Shiro and I will take care of you." I said gently reaching out to her.

"Keiko, you're so sweet. I'm glad you and Shiro are here."

In the following weeks, Mother seemed to feel better and slowly returned to her daily routine. She acted cheerful, but I could see the sadness in her eyes.

One afternoon, Mother asked if I would like to go shopping at the nearby market. Excited, I immediately called out to Shiro, "Let's go." Shiro came running to my side.

It was a lovely day. I was happy, and chatted all the way as we walked to the market. We crossed the road to the market's entrance and, suddenly, I heard a succession of high-pitched yelps. I quickly turned and saw Shiro lying on the side of the road. My loud screams of terror were muffled by the roar of the speeding truck that had struck Shiro just seconds ago.

Her white body was covered with blood and lay limp and still. For a second, I saw her body twitch, which gave me a glimmer of hope.

I tried to run towards her, but Mother pulled me back firmly. She held me and buried my face into her comforting body.

I could barely hear Mother saying, "No Keiko, don't go!"

"No, no. Shiro can't die!" I cried screaming her name.

I buried Shiro at the top of the hill behind our house. I promised that I would never forget her. I placed a large rock along with her favorite toys, rice candy, and wild flowers to mark her gravesite. I didn't think I could go on without her. The loneliness in my heart was unbearable.

How I missed her almond-shaped eyes, her circling dance, and her lick-lick-licks on my face. But, the hardest change was not having the warmth of her body next to mine as we huddled under the futon each night.

In the days that followed, Mother and I often walked to Shiro's grave and sat in front of the rock where she was buried.

"Keiko," she would say, "I know the sadness you are feeling now that Shiro is gone. I feel the same."

"Why did Kamisama take them away? Does he know how sad we feel?" I asked.

"Yes he knows. There is nothing we can do but accept the plan he has for our lives," she said, trying to comfort me.

"But, why such a cruel plan?" I whispered hopelessly.
"To make us stronger and better people," she explained.
I didn't understand.

CHAPTER 12:
PASSPORT

In **the American** Embassy's immigration office, a man with a stern expression sat behind the brown wooden desk. The room reminded me of a waiting room at a doctor's office. The linoleum floor, which was polished to a high shine, intimidated me. Living in a traditional Japanese home, I was used to tatami mats made of straw. The top half of the office door had tinted glass that was rough, like a bunch of stones. English words were written in bold, black letters.

Mother and I sat on stiff-backed chairs, opposite the man. Her eyes were fixated on her lap.

"Mrs. Esaki, what is your daughter's name?"

"Keiko Esaki," Mother replied.

"When and where was she born?" Mother looked nervous as she wrung her hands.

"October 28, 1940, in Kokura, Kyushu."

"Where were you born?"

"Auburn, Washington, in the United States of America."

"You are a citizen of the United States of America, correct?"

"Yes."

"Your daughter Keiko is ten years old and she is the child of an American mother and a Japanese national father?"

"Correct," replied Mother.

"Can she speak English?"

"She does not speak a word of English. She only speaks and writes in Japanese."

"Mrs. Esaki, what is your reason for seeking a passport for you and your daughter to travel abroad?"

"My mother lives in America and is getting on in years. I want to bring Keiko to meet her before it is too late," Mother said.

"How long are you planning to stay in the United States?"

"We want to stay for two months, July and August of 1951."

"I know you've been trying to obtain your passports for two years. I have not been able to get the permission to grant them to you. I will keep trying from my end, but there is only so much I can do. Orders come from a higher office."

Mother gave a big sigh. "Thank you, sir. Please don't give up on us. My mother will be disappointed if she is not able to see Keiko, a granddaughter she has never met."

After leaving the embassy office, Mother and I walked in the cold February weather to downtown Kokura. A mix of snowflakes flurried around us, creating a magical kaleidoscope as they dropped to the ground.

"Keiko, you must be chilled to your bones. Let's stop at the noodle shop across the street and have a bowl. It will give us energy to travel the rest of the way home."

"Oh, Mother, ure-shi!" I exclaimed. I realized my stomach was ready for the noodles and hot broth.

Inside the small noodle shop, a short and plump woman greeted us, *"Irrashaimase!"* Her hair was covered with a dark muslin cloth tied in the back, and her face was bright red from bending over the hot noodle broth that boiled in the big pot.

Mother and I sat on the long wooden bench and ordered our noodles. We slurped up the hot noodles and the broth and enjoyed the warmth that traveled throughout our bodies.

"Mother, does it snow in America?"

"Yes it does. When it snowed, Baachan, your grandmother in America, used to fix noodles just like this for me and my brothers and sisters."

"Who will I meet when we go to America?" I asked.

"Half of my brothers and sisters have passed away. You remember that my favorite older sister, Annie, died from childbirth a year ago. She left three boys, and, Yuriko, a girl cousin the same age as you. You will get along well with her. Annie was so happy when I gave birth to a baby girl only four months after she gave birth to Yuriko."

"You told me all the pretty hand-sewn dresses that came in the crate from America were sent to me by your older sister, Annie."

"Every time Annie sewed a dress for Yuriko, she always remembered to sew one for you too."

"Mother, do you miss her?"

"Yes, more than anyone can imagine."

She wiped the tears as they trickled down her cheeks.

"Baachan misses her too. That is the reason why you and I need to go to America to visit. When we go, you will meet your five boy cousins and Yuriko."

"I wish I had a sister."

"When you meet Yuriko, I am sure that she will become just like a sister to you. Annie told me Yuriko does not like being the only girl in the family."

"Do you think Yuriko will like me?"

"I know she will!"

We opened the door and hesitantly walked out into the damp weather to catch the trolley from downtown Kokura to Hiagari Machi.

The severe winter in Kyushu was coming to an end. Pale-colored buds began to form on the bare cherry tree branches.

I left school with Yoshiko after a long afternoon of practicing the relay race for the upcoming *Undoukai* (school's athletic day) that was scheduled in May. After saying goodbye to Yoshiko at her front gate, I ran the two blocks to my house.

"I'm home mother!" I raced up the concrete stairs leading to our front entry-way. My black-and-white school uniform felt damp.

Mother came running out to the doorway. "Keiko, good news! Our passports arrived in the mail today! We are going to America!"

"Really, Mother?"

"Keiko, now we can go shopping and buy gifts for your five boy cousins and something extra special for Yuriko!"

"Can we buy cameras made in Japan for the boys and a Hakata doll for Yuriko?"

"Of course. They will be so excited when they see the gifts."

When the weekend came, Mother and I went to downtown Kokura and spent the day shopping for gifts to take to my cousins and Baachan in America. We went from store to store to find the perfect gifts.

I still remember that Mother was chatty and looked happy during our shopping trip.

I was happy that we would never have to sit in the depressing immigration office room again.

CHAPTER 13:
FAREWELL TO JAPAN

Kimura sensei, Yoshiko, and I sat on a large rock in the corner of the school yard on this last day of school. The empty playground with its manicured shrubs reflected the orderliness of Japanese school life. It was hard to believe this building was in shambles only a short five years ago.

"Yoshiko and Keiko, I know you have been spending many hours studying for your middle-school entrance exam. I hope you will continue to work hard during summer vacation," said Kimura sensei.

"But Keiko will be traveling to America to visit her grandmother for two months. I will be lost without my study partner," said Yoshiko.

"Yes, I am aware of that. This is the reason why I wanted to talk to you both. We need to make a plan on how you two will continue your studies, Keiko in America and Yoshiko in Japan," Kimura sensei replied.

"I promise to keep up with my homework even though I will be in America. Yoshiko and I can exchange letters to encourage each other, right, Yoshiko?" I asked.

"We can do that but I'll still miss you terribly," replied Yoshiko.

"Remember, Keiko will only be gone for two months. Time will go by quickly and she will be back by the start of the new school year. Keiko, I am sure you will have a wonderful time getting to know your grandmother in America. Don't forget to save time for your studies though," said Kimura sensei.

"Sensei, I promise!" I said, trying to lighten Yoshiko's mood.

"Yoshiko, you will be fine. I'll invite you over to my house to practice calligraphy during vacation," said Kimura sensei.

"Keiko, I won't see you before you leave for America, so let's say goodbye," she said, as she held out her hands. Yoshiko and I reached for her. We locked our fingers with each other as we stood in a circle. Yoshiko's tears trickled down her cheeks. Kimura sensei took out her handkerchief and gently wiped the tears from Yoshiko's face.

Early in the morning, on a beautiful day in June, I rode the train with Mother and Father to Yokohama Bay. I could hardly contain my excitement, knowing that Mother and I would be boarding a large ship to begin our journey to a faraway land called America.

The train came to a slow stop. A large black-and-white sign that said "Yokohama Bay" was on the far side of the train track.

"Keiko and Fujiye, it's time to get off the train. You can carry the small suitcases and I will carry the big one," said Father.

"Be careful, Keiko. Hold onto the railing and step down carefully to the platform," Mother said. I could tell that Mother was just as anxious as I was.

Father hailed a taxi, and we rode the short distance to Yokohama Bay. As the taxi driver rolled onto the cement dock of Yokohama Bay, I gasped when I saw the largest ship I'd ever seen in my life.

"This is the ship we'll be taking. It's called the American Mail," said Mother.

I screamed, "Sugoi!" It was much bigger than I had imagined.

"Don't get too excited Keiko. I want you to be prepared for a long, rough trip.

We'll be on this ship for two weeks. The waves will be rough and some areas will be freezing cold."

I noticed Father was quiet. I saw that his jaw muscles were clenched tight. I stepped close to him and held out my hands. He lifted me up into his arms and gave me the tightest hug.

"Keiko, listen to me. I want you to be a good girl and mind your mother and your Baachan in America. I know you will be having a good time but don't slack off on your studies," he said.

"Don't worry, Father, I will do everything you told me to do."

"I will think of you every day and look forward to your return in two months," Father said. I nodded my head looking up to him.

"Be on the lookout for the books that I will send you. Goto-san, who owns the corner bookstand, will help me choose the right books. He knows exactly what you want," he said.

Father turned to Mother and said, "Fujiye, tell your mother I wish I could be there to meet her. Will you give her my best regards?"

Mother bowed her head and said, "Thank you, Zenichi. I will give her your message."

Mother gave me a gentle nudge, "Keiko, it's now time for us to board the ship." Mother and I started climbing up the steep metal steps to the entrance of this large ship. Just before entering, we looked down and waved our farewells to Father. He appeared small and lonely as he waved back, standing on the wooden dock of Yokohama Bay.

CHAPTER 14:
BAACHAN'S STORY
RENTON, WASHINGTON 1951

Baachan lived in the housing projects of Renton Highlands, a neighborhood just south of Seattle. Many Japanese families lived there after returning from the internment camps. Rows of look-alike houses, with various colors of wood siding, lined both sides of the road. The houses looked like giant match boxes painted in different pastel colors. I didn't dare go out and wander the streets, because recognizing her house would be impossible. I wondered why every house looked almost identical.

Baachan was a small woman. Her graying hair was pulled away from her round face and was tied into a small knot in the back of her head. The skin on her face had a golden glow, undoubtedly from the long hours she spent outside in her vegetable garden. She stood up straight and spoke her native Japanese language with a clear and strong voice. It was obvious to me that I needed to obey her and do what she asked me to do.

My boy cousins, Kiyo, 13, and Taka, 12, lived with Baachan. Yuki, my mother's younger sister, was an invalid and she lived there, too. Yuki had trouble walking, but was able to help Baachan with simple household tasks such as washing the dishes and sweeping the floor.

"Baachan, why do you have so many people living with you?" I asked as I helped wipe the dishes after she cooked breakfast for everyone. "Do Kiyo and Taka have a mother and father?"

"Kiyo and Taka lost their mother. Their father remarried and the woman my son, Chuck, married, didn't want the boys around. I felt sorry for them, so I told their father the boys could come live with me."

"What happened to Yuki? Why is she in a wheelchair?" I asked.

"Yuki is my youngest daughter. Back in 1938, there was an epidemic in the valley where Jiichan and I had a vegetable farm. At the time, Yuki was a little girl and was not able to fight off the high fever. She was never the same after that, so I take care of her, too," she replied.

"In Japan, the younger ones take care of the older people, but you are doing the opposite. Baachan, you are taking care of all the young ones," I said.

"Keiko, you must remember that life is not fair. We all have to deal with the life Kamisama gave us."

When the last dish was wiped and put away in the cupboard, Baachan motioned me to come and sit down at the table. "Let's sip some tea so we can continue our conversation," she said.

"Keiko, all is not bad. Kamisama brought you and Fujiye back to me," Baachan smiled as she reached out and held my hand.

"Baachan, Mother and I are here for only two months. After that, we're going back to Japan. What will you do after we leave for home?" I asked, feeling sorry for her.

Baachan suddenly changed the subject. Her voice was happy as she said, "Tomorrow, your only girl cousin, Yuriko, and her three brothers will be arriving from South Bend, Oregon, to meet you. Yuriko is only four months older than you. I know you two will become best of friends."

"Mother told me that Yuriko's mother died while giving birth to a baby."

"Annie was my oldest daughter. She was a strong mother and a good wife to her husband. She was giving birth to her fifth child when complications occurred. They couldn't stop the bleeding and she died, leaving behind her husband, Bob, Yuriko, and three boys—Robert, David, and Gary. Bob remarried in less than a year and life hasn't been easy for the kids. I was not happy he remarried so quickly after Annie passed away. Men sometimes do stupid things. They don't think that what they do can hurt their children. Annie's kids would be better off without their stepmother. I was willing to raise them, too," she scowled. I could sense she was not happy with Yuriko's father.

"I remember when Annie died, Baachan. I found Mother kneeling by her sister's photo, sobbing. She cried for weeks. Shiro and I didn't know how to help her."

"Your mother endured great suffering in Japan, too. Little did I know that Japan and America would enter into World War II. If I had known that, I would never have sent her to Japan to live with my brother and his wife. They were childless and begged me to send them one of my children so their last name Esaki could be carried on long after they died," Baachan said.

"My Ojiichan in Kokura was your brother?" I exclaimed.

"Yes, the man who you called Ojiichan was my older brother. He held a prestigious position as the Chief of Police in Kokura. He could not imagine that his famous last name, Esaki, could possibly disappear from history after he died. He wanted me to send him a son, but that was out of the question. My husband and I needed all the boys to help with the farm. My brother finally settled for a girl. His plan was to have your mother marry a man who would take the Esaki name."

I listened in silence, holding my breath, as Baachan told me stories I had never heard before. Memories of Ojiichan flooded my mind. For the first time, I understood how my father, Zenichi, came to marry Mother and take on the name "Esaki" to carry on Ojiichan's name.

"Keiko, I think this is enough for today. Yuriko and her brothers will be coming tomorrow so help me clean up the house and cook a big meal. There will be five active boys in this house and they are a hungry brood!" Baachan warned.

The next day, Kiyo and Taka could hardly hold back their excitement as they waited for their boy cousins — Robert, David, and Gary — to arrive. Baachan and I made onigiri rice balls and a big pot of soup for the cousins.

All of a sudden, the front door burst open, and my cousins from South Bend came running in. The boys immediately started to wrestle with each other, hooting and hollering in delight.

"Settle down boys! You have guests here who traveled all the way from Japan,"

Baachan said in her stern voice.

"Meet your Aunt Fujiye and cousin Keiko. They brought many wonderful gifts for you." The boys suddenly became quiet, waiting for the gifts that Mother and I brought for them.

I gave each of the boys a camera, a model car, and a Japanese boy's game.

"Yuriko, come and meet Keiko," said Baachan.

Yuriko stepped forward with a shy smile on her face. She was no stranger to me because Mother had shown me many photos of Yuriko and her mother, Annie.

I gave Yuriko her special girl's omiyage of a traditional Hakata doll, origami papers, pens, and pencils. Yuriko squealed with delight. After that, we immediately became best friends, even though neither one of us spoke the other's language. We spent every minute of that day together. We made dresses for paper dolls, played with the games I brought from Japan, and helped Baachan tend to her vegetable garden.

   As Mother tucked me into bed that night, she said, "Keiko, your dream has finally came true. You found the sister you have always longed for. Are you happy?" I nodded my head and smiled as I quickly dozed off to sleep.

CHAPTER 15:
SHOPPING ADVENTURE

My first shopping adventure in America. I could hardly contain my excitement as I rode the bus to downtown Seattle. Yuriko and I sat together. Baachan and Mother sat behind us. I couldn't believe the large, gray buildings that lined both sides of the street. I was used to seeing narrow streets lined with lots of little shops with colorful banners flying about in the air. Many shop owners also stood outside their stores to encourage shoppers to come in.

"Everything is so big in America," I said to Baachan.

"Of course. America is a big country compared to Japan," she replied.

The bus driver hollered, "Next stop is Third Avenue and Pine!"

"Keiko and Yuriko, we will be getting off shortly, so please stand up and walk to the front of the bus. Make sure you hang on to the poles. I don't want you to fall," directed Mother. Yuriko and I stood up and walked to the front, hanging tightly onto the metal poles that stood on both sides of the center aisle. The bus suddenly came to a stop, jolting us all backwards. After we recovered, we stepped off the bus the minute the door flew open.

Baachan pointed at the large building in front of us and said, "This is Penney's department store. Let's go inside and take a look." We obediently followed her and entered through the large glass double door that led into the store. Inside were rows of shiny glass display cases with jewelry and watches. Then came more cases with lipsticks, powder, and brightly colored nail polishes.

"Wow, I've never seen so many nail polishes before. Baachan, can I have one?" I asked.

"I want the pink one!" exclaimed Yuriko.

"Keiko and Yuriko, I don't want you to ever buy these bright-colored nail polishes. Only flashy street girls wear them. You don't want anyone to think you're not a nice girl do you?" Baachan lectured with a stern face.

"Listen to her and remember what she is telling you," Mother echoed. It seemed that she always agreed with Baachan. I wondered why she never took my side.

"Let's go to the girl's clothing section downstairs. I will buy each of you a matching outfit," Baachan said in her upbeat voice. We followed her down the escalator.

We came to a section of the store where there were racks of young girls' clothing. The circular racks were filled with hanging outfits in pink, purple, blue, and yellow.

"Look Keiko, there are cute peddle-pusher pants with plaid tops. You can try on the pink set and I'll try on the blue," Yuriko exclaimed.

"Girls, go to the dressing room and try them on. Then come out and show Obaachan and me, so we can see if they look good on you," said Mother. When we came out of the dressing room wearing our pink and blue outfits, Baachan exclaimed, "I like those on you girls. Keiko, you now look like an American girl!"

We walked out of Penney's department store with each of us holding a bag—Yuriko with the blue outfit and me with the pink set. "Now we can be like real sisters, Keiko; we have matching outfits!" Yuriko and I giggled with delight as we walked down the street to another large building.

"This is Kress's Dime Store. Wait until you see this store, Keiko. You will see some of the things I sent to Japan for you," said Baachan.

We stepped into the store, which was huge. The shelves and glass cases were filled with everything imaginable. It was almost too much for my eyes to absorb.

"Ohh," I gasped.

As we walked through the store, I saw things that were familiar to me—boxes of packaged gum, embroidery kits, colored crayons, and coloring books.

"Baachan, did you buy everything you sent to me from this store?" I asked.

"Yes, I came here every week, looking for something I thought you might like. I knew you didn't have much in Japan after the war. I wanted you to have the same experiences that American children had and thought that you could do that with the care packages I sent you."

As we turned the corner, I saw her—the life-sized baby doll with the big eyes and the long eyelashes. I took her carefully off the shelf. When

I turned her upside-down, she cried "Mama, Mama." The cry of the doll brought back bittersweet memories of Japan. I saw myself in Kokura, playing with the doll as Shiro sat next to me. I remembered her barking and whimpering every time the doll cried. I wished Shiro was here with me in America.

"There is one more thing I want you to see Keiko," Baachan said, as she motioned me toward the back of the store. We followed her down the long aisle and turned the corner. Standing against a wall was a large machine with a see-through window.

Yuriko said, "Look, Keiko. This is called a popcorn machine. See how the corn kernels are puffing up as they bounce around the machine and are covered with butter?" I stepped closer to the machine to watch the corn pop as it flew about in the machine.

"Do you remember I sent you popcorn?" Baachan asked.

Suddenly, I was surrounded by the strong aroma of the butter, salt, and popcorn.

"Baachan, now I know. This is the smell of America!"

CHAPTER 16:
THE TRUTH

I **could hear voices** in the distance. Mari, Yoshiko, and Hideki were calling me, "Keiko, are you done with supper? Come down to the street. We are waiting for you. Let's go and catch fireflies. They're out tonight!"

I jumped up from the dinner table and tried to run. My legs wouldn't move. I panicked. "I'm trying to come, but I can't move!" I screamed out.

The voices of my friends continued, "Hurry Keiko, the fireflies will be gone!"

"I'm trying!"

Suddenly, I felt a hand on my shoulder shaking me. When I opened my eyes, Mother stood over me. "Are you all right, Keiko? You were screaming and struggling. Were you having a bad dream?"

"Mari, Yoshiko, and Hideki were calling me, but I couldn't go to meet them because my legs wouldn't move," I replied, still groggy from sleep.

"Keiko, you are in America now. Don't think about your friends in Japan so much. Try to enjoy all that America has to offer. Baachan and your cousins are happy that you came."

"I miss my friends."

"Let's cheer up! I have a plan to take you someplace very special today," Mother said, using her upbeat voice.

"Where are we going?" I asked.

"It's a surprise, but I am sure that you will like it," she said with a twinkle in her eyes.

"May I wear the new outfit Baachan bought me yesterday?" I asked, rubbing the sleep out of my eyes.

"Yes, the pink-checkered top and the white cropped pants looked good on you," said Mother.

I quickly got out of bed and got dressed.

Mother and I walked to the bus stop, which was a block away from Baachan's house. When the bus came, we walked up the four steps and paid our fare. Unlike the crowded buses in Japan, this bus was almost empty, with only a few people sitting in the seats.

After a short ride, the bus came to a stop in front of a brown, brick, one-story building. "We've arrived, Keiko," Mother said.

As we crossed the street and walked toward the building, I saw the American flag with its red, white, and blue colors waving gallantly in the air. I immediately stood at attention and admired the bright-colored flag against the pale blue sky.

Mother stopped in front of the big double doors of the building and said, "We are about to enter a library. You will love what's inside!"

As we quietly stepped in, I saw a huge room lined with wooden shelves. Each row was tightly packed with books of all sizes. A few people leisurely walked between the aisles, looking at and touching the books. I stared in amazement. I had never seen so many books under one roof.

"Mother, how can people in America buy all these books?" I asked.

"They don't have to buy them. They can check out the books for free and read them at home. When they are finished reading them, they return the books, and more books can be checked out," Mother replied.

"Are the books really free?" I questioned.

"Remember how I limited your reading in Japan? That's because I had to buy each of the books for you. You read so quickly, I couldn't afford to buy all the books you wanted."

"I understand, Mother, but why did you bring me here? You know that I can't read or speak in English," I said, raising my voice in frustration.

"Sh-h-h-h…you need to keep your voice down. The librarian is looking at us," Mother whispered.

I looked at the tall American woman standing behind the counter. Her eyes and lips were pale. Her sandy-colored hair seemed to blend right into her white skin. She was looking at me with a stern expression on her face.

"Let's go over there so I can explain why I brought you here." Mother led me to a small table at the far corner of the room. She sat in the chair and quickly motioned for me to sit next to her.

When I sat down, she looked at me with a serious expression on her face. "It's okay that you aren't able to read right now. Soon, you will be able to read every book in this room. We can start today by checking out a few books on American history. I can help you to read the famous story of

George Washington, America's first president."

"How can I learn to read in two months?" I asked. "Soon, we will be leaving America to go back to Japan."

"Keiko, this is what I wanted to tell you. We won't be going back to Japan. We will be staying in America," Mother said.

"You are lying to me! I have to go back to Japan! My teachers and friends are waiting for me. I need to study for the sixth grade exam. And, I miss Father."

"Keiko, there is something you don't know. I've kept this a secret, but it's time you learned the truth." Mother took a deep breath and said, "Zenichi, the man you call Father, is not your real father."

My body started to shake and everything around me began to spin. I jumped up and ran to the entryway. Flying through the door, I screamed "Liar, liar!"

Mother, who was close behind, grabbed my arm and held me close.

"Please forgive me Keiko. I have kept a terrible secret from you."

"You're a liar, I hate you!" I struggled to get away. "Let me go!" I screamed, "Let me go!"

She wouldn't let go. "Keiko, I'm sorry, so sorry." She held me tightly until I became still.

"Please come to the bench and sit down. I will tell you the whole story," she pleaded.

Mother led me to the shade of a large tree. She gently sat me down.

"Your real father's name was Tatsunosuke Tadamatsu. He died in the Philippine Islands while fighting for the Japanese Navy. It was shortly after you were born," she said. "Do you remember the large photo of a young Navy officer that hung on the wall at Obaachan's house in Fukuoka? She told you he was your father and you thought she was lying. Remember? She was telling you the truth, Keiko. He was her son and your father. Tatsunosuke was my husband. I loved him very much," Mother revealed.

"So everyone was lying to me, except Obaachan in Fukuoka, who tried to tell me the truth. And I called her a liar."

"Don't feel badly. You didn't know any better; you only knew what was told to you. On his death bed, Ojiichan made me promise that you would grow up knowing Zenichi as your father."

"Why would Ojiichan want to deceive me?" I asked.

"It's a long story. Ojiichan was my mother's older brother. My mother and father immigrated to the United States many years ago. They came here with the hope of finding a better life."

"Why? Was their life bad in Japan?"

"Baachan's husband, my father, was the youngest son of three brothers. In Japan, the oldest son receives all the family possessions when their parents die. Japan was going through an economic hardship, and he was faced with the reality of a hopeless future. That's when he heard from others that America was a land of many opportunities and made up his mind to settle here with his young wife.

"The man you knew in Kokura as Ojiichan was my uncle. He was Baachan's older brother. Ojiichan and his wife were childless. He was the Chief of Police in Kokura and couldn't bear the thought of dying with no one to inherit his wealth or carry on the Esaki name. He wrote to my mother and asked her to send one of her five children to Japan. Out of respect for her older brother, Baachan had no choice but to do as he asked."

Mother continued, "He wanted a son, but Baachan's husband refused. Boys are valuable to farmers. They needed strong boys to help on the farm."

"Obaachan told me something like that before. You were the one your mother and father decided to send to Japan?"

"Yes. Ojiichan decided having a girl would be better than having no one. His plan was to arrange a marriage where the groom would change his last name to Esaki. That way, he would be assured his respected name would be carried forth by his grandchildren.

"Did he find my real father, Tatsunosuke for you?"

"No, it was unfortunate for Ojiichan that I met your father on my own. Tatsunosuke was a detective in the Police Department. He interrogated foreigners who committed crimes in Japan. Since I could speak English and Japanese, he asked me to be his interpreter."

"So you fell in love with Tatsunosuke?"

"Yes. When Tatsunosuke asked Ojiichan for my hand, he said yes, but only under one condition. He would have to take on the Esaki name. Tatsunosuke's parents refused to give up their son to become an Esaki. They were proud of their own name, Tadamatsu, a name that was passed down from their samurai family.

"Ojiichan realized your father and I were deeply in love and we were not going to let anyone get in our way. Finally, he and Tatsunosuke's parents came to an agreement that I would take on the Tadamatsu name.

Our first born child, which is you, would be a Tadamatsu but the second born child going forward would take the Esaki name."

I was shocked by the story Mother was telling me. It sounded like a fictional Japanese drama.

"You and Tatsunosuke married, but what happened after that, Mother? Your last name and mine is Esaki, not Tadamatsu," I asked.

"Your father and I married in 1939. World War II began in 1941 when the Japanese Air Force launched a surprise attack on Pearl Harbor. Over 3,500 Americans were killed or wounded in two waves of terrifying attacks. In addition, many aircraft were destroyed and battleships were sunk, killing thousands of American servicemen. An all-out war between Japan and America began that took a terrible toll on both countries."

"Mother, how terrible for you! Your parents, sisters, and brothers were in America and Japan was at war with your country?"

"Yes, I was torn between two countries. My family in America suffered, too. After Japan attacked Pearl Harbor, all Japanese residing on the West Coast were sent to internment camps. My parents, forced to leave their vegetable farming business in Auburn, lost everything while they were in camp."

"I remember the air raids and evacuations in the underground caves in Japan," I said, not wanting to think about those terrifying days again.

"Meanwhile, in Japan, your father was very happy when he found out that I was pregnant with you, our first child. When you came into the world, he doted on you like no one I have ever seen. But, the war tore our lives apart. The happy days came to an abrupt end when he was drafted into the Japanese Navy. He was sent to the Philippine Islands to fight for the Emperor of Japan.

When you were eight-months old, I received a letter from the Japanese Navy informing me that your father had been killed fighting for his country." Mother's voice and body began to shake as she tried to fight back her tears.

"Oh, Mother, how sad you must have felt," I said.

After sitting for a few minutes in silence, Mother regained her composure. She continued, "That is when Ojiichan took us back to his family. Our last name was changed from Tadamatsu to Esaki at that time. Shortly after your first birthday, Ojiichan found a young police officer who worked for the Kokura Police Department, and he decided that we should marry. He said that I needed a husband, and you, a father, to survive this difficult time of war. This man was Zenichi, who you believed was your father.

"Did you love him, Mother?" I questioned.

"I had no natural affection for Zenichi when Ojiichan brought him home. I realized Ojiichan was happy because Zenichi, unlike Tatsunosuke, did not come from a proud family. He came to Kokura from a small village located in the northern coast of Kokura. Zenichi's first wife died during childbirth. Zenichi left his son to be cared for by his mother and relatives and ventured to the city to start a new life. Of course he was happy when Ojiichan offered him my hand. He saw that by taking the Esaki name, he would become heir to Ojiichan's wealth.

"Instead of you, Mother?" I questioned.

"Yes, a woman in Japan is nothing without a man. It is the man in the family who is given all the power to control the family's wealth."

"Then, what happened?" I asked.

"Zenichi was drafted into the army shortly after we married. Later that year, I received news that he was captured and was a prisoner of war in Manchuria. This is the reason why you have no memory of ever having a father until Zenichi returned. You were a baby and your time with both of your fathers was so brief."

"Did you hear about Zenichi after he was captured?"

"Not a word. I was told to assume that he was dead because no one would be able to survive the brutal treatment in captivity as a POW," said Mother. "Keiko, that is why I was surprised when I got the word that Zenichi would be coming home. Remember the day that you and I went to the Kokura station to meet him and I forced you to run up and hug him?"

I nodded my head, remembering that strange day.

"Keiko, you must know that I was miserable living with Zenichi after he came back from Manchuria. He was a changed man. When he drank, his hatred toward Americans came out, and he took his anger out on me. He hated that I worked at the American army base. He became jealous of everyone that I came in contact with, including my Japanese-American co-workers, who came from the United States, just like me. I felt so badly that you had to witness all those times when Zenichi was violent with rage. You had no one to turn to except your dog, Shiro."

I began to remember those times when Shiro and I sat hovering outside the door, not knowing what to do. The warmth from Shiro's body was the only thing that gave me comfort.

"Mother, you seemed happy when you were with the Japanese-American friends who worked with you," I recalled.

"That's because I felt comfortable with them. I was never able to make friends with many Japanese women. Most of them despised the fact that I came from America and considered me a traitor."

"I felt badly when I saw them spitting at you on the street."

Mother continued, "The only relatives I had were your real father's family in Fukuoka, but we were not on good terms. Ojiichan made them sign a contract immediately after we got the news that Tatsunosuke had died. It stated that you and I would be taken back to the Esaki family. The Tadamatsu family would be allowed to see you for two weeks every summer, but under one condition. They could never tell you that Tatsunosuke was your real father."

"Now I understand why Obaachan spent so much time with me, talking about her son, Tatsunosuke," I said, remembering that strange afternoon in Fukuoka when Obaachan called me "granddaughter" and told me that Tatsunosuke was my father.

"You were led to believe that everyone in the Tadamatsu family were distant relatives. Of course they were angry that you and I were abruptly taken away from their family after Tatsunosuke died."

"Mother, you went through a lot," I whispered, reaching out for her hand.

"I had no choice but to bring you to America. I told Zenichi I wanted to bring you here for two months so you could visit with Baachan before she died. If I had told him the truth, he would never let us come. I left Japan with only two suitcases—one for you and one for me. I left behind all of Ojiichan's wealth with Zenichi, but I didn't mind because freedom from him meant everything to me."

"Why didn't you let me finish my sixth-grade and give me a chance to take the exam to enter the middle school of my choice?" I asked.

"Because you will be turning twelve years old next year. A child born abroad by an American woman is automatically granted two citizenships, one Japanese and one American. However, once the child turns twelve, she must claim a citizenship in only one country. Keiko, it's always been my plan to bring you back to America to raise you here.

"You may not be happy now, but a day will come when you'll appreciate the decision I made. You are passionate and industrious, admirable traits that you inherited from your Father. I didn't want to see you become someone's puppet like me. I wanted you to grow up free and to have a chance to reach your full potential."

Mother took my hands and squeezed them tightly. "Keiko, do you know that you are the luckiest girl who grew up in the luckiest city? You were destined to die in Kokura, instead, you are alive."

"What are you saying Mother?"

"America had three target cities in Japan where they planned to drop the atomic bombs. These nuclear bombs were so horrific and destructive that whole cities were flattened and thousands of people burned to death within minutes after the bombs hit the ground. These air attacks were planned as a final blow to Japan so that it would surrender. The first attack targeted the city of Hiroshima in 1945. You were five years old at that time. A few days after the Hiroshima attack, the second atomic bomb was scheduled to be dropped on Kokura."

"Why in Kokura?"

"America made a decision to target our city because we had a large weapons manufacturing plant. On the morning of August 9, 1945, an American war plane loaded with the atomic bomb flew over Kokura. If the pilot had released the bomb as planned, you and I wouldn't be alive today."

"What happened? Why didn't they drop the bomb over Kokura?" I asked, with growing suspense.

"It was a cloudy day. The city was hazy with smoke from the smaller bombing attacks that had been going on for weeks. The pilots and the crew were not able to get a clear view of the city. They circled over Kokura five times, waiting to get a better view of the city. They had strict orders not to drop the bomb unless they had at least seventy percent visibility of the targeted area. On their sixth circle over the city, the visibility was still poor. By then, their fuel supply was getting low. They were given orders to fly to the nearby city of Nagasaki on the western coast of Kyushu. The bomb was dropped there, destroying the city and killing thousands of innocent people.

"I know Nagasaki. That's where we went to visit the seaside one summer. I loved the scenic trails."

"Yes, it's beautiful now," agreed Mother. "But, at that time, it was a devastating blow to Japan. Most of Nagasaki was destroyed beyond recognition and many of its people burned to death. If you go to Hiroshima and Nagasaki today, it is haunting. But both cities now have beautiful memorial sites to honor the people who lost their lives."

"Are you telling me that I am alive today because of the poor weather conditions and that thousands of innocent people in Nagasaki died in my place?"

"Yes, that is the reason I called you the luckiest girl in the luckiest city," Mother said with a smile on her face.

My mind was spinning after hearing all the details of our lives. I knew what Mother had told me was the truth.

"Keiko, you are indeed a special girl. Your life was spared. Take your passion for Japan and focus it on America. Study hard and learn English. Do something good for the world. You owe it to your father, who gave his life in the war. You owe it to all of those who died from the horrible bombings."

For the first time, I understood the suffering inflicted on the lives of people, both in Japan and America.

"Let's go home, Mother. I want to tell Baachan that I'm staying in America."

We walked to the bus stop in silence, holding hands.

CHAPTER 17:
SURVIVOR

I don't belong here. Dirty school grounds, books marked with scribbles, rude students with brown and blond hair. What am I doing here?

It had been three months since I was thrust into the fifth-grade class at Highland Elementary School. I sat in class, in total silence, not understanding very much that was being spoken. I didn't have even a friend to play with during recess. Even though I was totally isolated, I did my best to at least follow Mrs. Baldwin's orders. I saw that she was frustrated and didn't know what to do with a student who only understood and spoke the Japanese language.

After a few weeks, Mrs. Baldwin approached me before class started and said, "I need to talk to you about something. Can you step into my office?"

I followed her obediently. "Your Japanese name, Keiko, has been difficult to pronounce for the students in your class. What do you think about changing it to 'Kay'? It will be much easier for students to call you with the correct pronunciation if you have an American name. Is that okay with you?"

I nodded my head and answered, "Yes, Mrs. Baldwin."

Finally, the day came when Mrs. Baldwin pointed me out in the class. She asked, "Kay, can you answer a simple question for me?" Every eye in the room turned to look at me. I'm sure if someone had dropped a pin, everyone would have heard it.

My face felt hot and flushed. I felt like hundreds of eyes were piercing through my body. I took a deep breath and nodded my head, "Yes, Mrs. Baldwin."

"Kay, we are studying about the state of Texas. Agriculture is very rich there. Can you tell me what they grow in Texas?"

I stared intently at her and was sure that my eyes were blank, as if they were saying, "I don't know what you are talking about."

She paused for few moments, waiting for me to reply. When I didn't respond, she went on to say, "Okay, let me give you a hint. The color is white." Again, I didn't understand what she meant. I had a sudden urge to run out of the room, but I forced myself to stay seated. "Let me give you another hint. It's fluffy. When you blow on it, it floats away." At that point, I raised my hand and shouted, "Snow!"

The whole room broke out in laughter. The teacher hushed the students and said, "The answer I was looking for is cotton." The students resumed laughing again.

I sat there with tears streaming down my face. I was not used to being laughed at. Why was I being subjected to this humiliating situation when I had been a shining student at the top of my class in Japan?

The closing school bell rang. As I stood up from my desk to leave the room, Mrs. Baldwin came over. She said, "Kay, I'm sorry you had to go through a hard time in class today. I know how difficult it must be for you to start all over in another country." I nodded, trying to hold back the tears that seemed so close to running down my face.

"I want to make sure that you won't be embarrassed again. Let me explain your assignment for tomorrow's art class. We will be drawing and coloring pictures for our upcoming Christmas holiday. It's a contest. The chosen artwork will be posted on the bulletin board in our school lunchroom. If you have crayons or colored pencils, please bring them with you to class. Do you understand what I just said?"

I nodded my head and replied, "Yes, Teacher."

The minute I arrived home, I ran into the bedroom and flopped myself on the bed and cried. Mother came in and asked, "Keiko, what's wrong, why are you crying?"

"I'm not going back to school, and you can't make me!" I screamed, tears running down my burning cheeks.

"Tell me what happened that made you so upset," Mother asked as she gently stroked my head.

"All the kids are mean and they laugh at me because I don't understand or speak their language. They treat me like I'm dumb. But, I am not, Mother!" I blurted out, as my body shook with anger. "I hate America. I want to go home to Japan. I miss my teachers and friends. They are waiting for me to come back."

"Keiko, I know how much you miss Japan, but we aren't going back. I promise, if you accept humility and try hard in school, your life will improve. I know you can do it. You are bright and you have good study habits." I stood up and let Mother wipe my tears away.

I walked over to the closet and took out the gray suitcase I brought from Japan. When I opened its cover, I found the art supplies that I used in Japan. Old memories returned. I had previously been selected to represent our school in the citywide art contest. My artwork was often displayed in the largest department store in the city of Kokura. I carefully took out the oil paint and the watercolor set and touched them. Memories overwhelmed me with sadness. It had been over six months since I painted a landscape, flowers, or a bowl of neatly arranged fruit, sitting side by side with art contestants from other schools in the region.

The next day, Mrs. Baldwin stood in front of the class and announced, "Students, do you remember what I said we are going to do in class today? We will be drawing and coloring Christmas objects. You may have your choice of what you would like to draw—Santa Claus, Christmas trees, snow-covered villages, or anything else related to winter or the holidays."

The students showed their excitement by yelling in unison, "Yeah!"

"If your artwork is chosen by Mr. Hall, our principal, you will have a chance for the whole school to see your talent. The winning artwork will be posted on the lunchroom's bulletin board. Good luck!"

Everyone in the class took out their boxes of crayons and began drawing and coloring their artwork.

I quietly took my watercolor set and drew a snowy forest scene where deer roamed. I closed my eyes and imagined I was in a Japanese forest in the winter time. I could smell the scent of the pine trees in the calm and pristine wooded area. I drew, colored, and shaded the trees. I added slender silhouettes of the roaming deer. The scene was unfolding and coming alive on the paper that lay in front of me. I had not had a feeling like this since I left Japan.

"Students, it's time to stop working. Please hold up your artwork so everyone can see."

I looked at the scribbled red Santa Claus figures and reindeers other students drew, and I saw how different my work was. Everyone drew figures with stick limbs. They were all brightly-colored with red and green crayons. I was the only one who painted a snowy forest scene that required creating many muted shades with watercolors.

When I held up my artwork, Mrs. Baldwin came walking to my desk and exclaimed, "Where did you learn to draw and color like this?"

All the students looked at my artwork and, in unison, exclaimed,

"Wow!"

I knew I had made up for the humiliation of replying "snow" in yesterday's geography class.

My forest scene was chosen as the first place winner by Mr. Hall. He had it framed and hung on the wall of the lunchroom. The sign next to the painting read, "Painting by Kay Esaki, First Place Winner."

I ran home after school. I flung open the door to Baachan's house.

"Keiko, you're home," Mother greeted me.

"Mother, I'm sorry that I've given you so much trouble. I'm ready to put all of my effort into becoming a good student in America. You will see."

"Keiko, why this sudden change of attitude?"

"Mother, I found out today that I can be good at something, even if I can't speak or write English. The snow scene I drew in class today won first place in the student art contest!"

"I'm not surprised. I knew all along that this would eventually happen." Mother looked pleased and beamed with pride.

"That's not all, Mother. Mr. Hall, our principal, called me to his office today and told me how much he loved my artwork. He then asked me if I would like to draw a large mural on the lunchroom wall!"

Mother's eyes were wet with tears. She came over and held me tight. Her voice trembled as she said, "Your father would be so proud of you, Keiko. You went through hard times in Japan, but you learned some valuable lessons as well. No one will be able to take your good study habits and your kind heart away from you."

"Mother, I will try very hard to become a good student in America."

From that day forward, I often recalled Mother's wise words that gave me the courage and focus as I continued to grow in America:

"Keiko, you are a special girl. Your life was spared. Take your passion for Japan and focus it on America. Study hard and learn English. Do something good for the world. You owe it to your father who gave his life in the war. You owe it to everyone who died from those horrible bombings."

To this day, as I live my life in America, her teachings have been the guiding force within me. Remembering her constant sacrifices, selfless suffering, and positive influences has been the impetus for establishing the firm foundation I built for my life and career.

For that, I will be forever grateful.

EPILOGUE

I struggled for many years to assimilate into the American culture, constantly searching to find a sense of belonging. Mother never talked about Japan. She wanted me to assimilate myself into the American culture.

Two years after we arrived in America, Mother revealed another secret to me.

She had contracted tuberculosis in Japan while living through the many hardships of the war. For the next fifteen years, she was incapacitated with the disease, forcing me to raise myself with the help of Baachan. Again, I was left in the position of worrying about Mother.

Mother finally succumbed and passed away from complications of the disease when I was twenty-eight. When she died, I felt a complete loss of my past and self identity. I was determined, however, to find my life's purpose and do whatever positive things I could to honor Mother's personal sacrifices.

At the age of thirty-six, I traveled to Japan to reconnect with the people in my past. I had a tearful and joyous reunion with Zenichi (my stepfather), Uncle Torao (my father's brother) and my cousins. I was told that Obaachan (my paternal grandmother) had passed away a year ago. Her dying wish was to find me again.

The memory of Shiro never left me. I was able to return to Kokura and visit her grave. The rock was gone, but I knew exactly where I had buried her. As I stood and recalled the incident leading to her death, the overwhelming pain that I felt was as intense as the day it happened. To this day, I continue to love and respect animals for their ability to comfort humans during their personal times of hardship.

After I returned to America, I was finally able to call this country my home. I was proud. It felt good, like I actually belonged here. Instead of feeling ashamed that I came from Japan, I felt honored that I was able to draw from not one, but two extremely rich cultures. I was anxious and ready to pursue a purpose-driven life ... to create a better world. Although my path and direction is much clearer now, there is still much to be accomplished toward that end.

GLOSSARY

"Arigatou" – "Thank you."

"Arigatou, Obasan" – Thank you, lady (a name for a woman who is older).

Bachi – punishment, curse or retribution.

Bon Odori – A Buddhist custom to honor the spirits of one's ancestors. Spirits of the ancestors are believed to revisit the household altars. Traditionally includes a dance festival, known as *Bon-Odori*.

"Chi-chi-pa-pa-chi-pa-pa... suzume-no-gakkou-no-sensei-wa, muchi-o-furi-furi-chi-pa-pa" – A favorite Japanese children's song that tells the story of the sparrow school. "A sparrow teacher chirps and chirps, swinging her whip as she teaches sparrow students."

"Daijobu, Arigato" – "I am all right. Thank you."

Densha – Trolley.

"Doudesuka?" – "How are you doing?"

"Dou-itashi-mashite" – "You are welcome."

Fukuoka no Obaachan – Grandmother who lives in the city of Fukuoka.
SEE ALSO FIG. 01: *Kyushu Map*

Gaman – Hold yourself back and maintain self-control.

Genkan – Entryway to the house. The primary function of the genkan is for the removal of shoes and the dirt on the shoes before entering the main part of the house.

Geta – A traditional wooden footwear resembling thongs, usually worn with a kimono.

Hakama – Traditional Japanese clothing for men. It is tied at the waist, has divided legs and hangs to the ankles.

"Hai, wakarimashita" – Yes, I understand.

Hakata doll – Traditional clay dolls, called Hakata ningyou, which was named after Hakata in Fukuoka prefecture.

Hiagari machi – Hiagari city.

Hiagari Shougakkou – A grade school that Keiko attended in Kokura.

"Iie" – "No."

"Ikimashou" – "Let's go."

"Irashai mase" – "Welcome."

Jiichan – Informal way of saying Grandpa.
SEE ALSO *Ojiichan*

Kamaboko – Fish cake. A Japanese processed seafood product. Formed into distinctive loafs and steamed until firm. They are used in many dishes such as noodles and salads.

Kami-sama – Japanese god.

Kanji – There are three levels that are used in the Japanese writing system. They are *Katakana* (children start with this elementary form of writing), then move up to learn the Hiragana. *Kanji* is the most advanced level of writing and reading.

Karuta – Japanese cards. The basic idea of a karuta game is to be able to quickly determine which card out of an array of cards is required and then to grab the card before it is grabbed by an opponent.

Kojiki – Homeless person.

Kokura – City situated in the northern tip of Kyushu. This city is known for its ancient castles. During World War II, the Koshikawa Arsenal, a manufacturing plant for war weapons, was situated there. Kokura was a target city where American planes were scheduled to drop the atomic bomb on August 9, 1945. Kokura is called the "lucky city" because the bomb was dropped on Nagasaki instead.
SEE ALSO FIG. 01: *Kyushu Map*

Konnichi-wa – A salutation meaning, it's a good day.

Kotatsu – A heating element underneath a small table covered with a quilt to keep the heat from escaping. Japanese homes did not have central heating units so they depended on the heat from kotatsu to keep them warm in the winter months.

Kozou – Small trouble maker.

Kurume – A city in Fukuoka Prefecture. Kurume is located south of Kokura. Fujiye's uncle lived in Kurume.
SEE ALSO FIG. 01: *Kyushu Map*

Kyushu – The third largest island in Japan and most southwesterly of its four main islands.
SEE ALSO FIG. 01: *Kyushu Map*

Mago-musume – Granddaughter.

Manju – Traditional Japanese confectionary. Its outer covering is made from rice or wheat flour.

Nagasaki – A peaceful port city located southwest of Kokura. The second atomic bomb on Japan (after Hiroshima) was dropped on Nagasaki and nearly wiped out the city and its population on August 9, 1945.
SEE ALSO FIG. 01: *Kyushu Map*

Nawatobi – Jump rope game. The rope is held by two children. As they swing the rope in a circle-like fashion, the third child hops in and jumps through the rope.

Obaachan – Grandma. An endearing way to express closeness to one's Grandmother.

FIG. 01: KYUSHU MAP

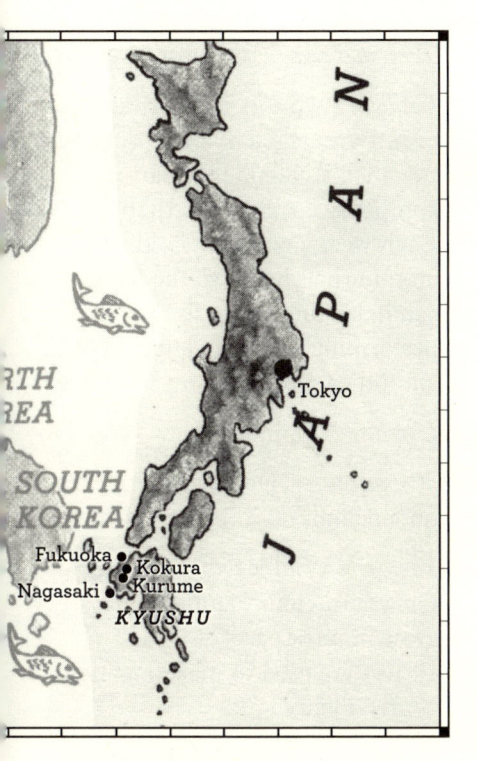

Obasan – Aunt or an older woman.

Obon – Japanese Buddhist custom to honor the spirits of one's ancestors. In the evenings, yukata clad men and women participate in the *bon odori* (dance) to celebrate the return of the dead. This celebration takes place in the late summer.
SEE ALSO *Bon Odori*

Ohajiki – Flat disks made of glass. Children will spill a handful on the *tatami* mat and push them with their fingers. When a pair collides, then the player is allowed to keep them. The person who ends up with the most disks at the end of the game is the winner.

Ojiichan – Children use this endearing term for "grandpa."

"*Ojiichan, omizu wa dou desuka?*" – "Grandpa, would you like some water?"

"*Ojiichan, oyasumi.*" – "Good night, Grandpa."

Ojisan – A formal name for elderly man.

Ojuzu – Buddhist prayer beads.

Okaachan – Children use this endearing term for "mommy."

Okaeri-nasai – Welcome home.

Omiyage – Souvenir one brings on a trip from another place, while temi-yage are thank you gifts given when visiting a friend or relative's home. Japanese tourists tend to buy lots of souvenirs for their friends, relatives and co-workers.

Onigiri – Hand-made balls of rice that are wrapped in seaweed. Some contain pickled *ume* (miniature plums).

Otedama – Small hand-sewn fabric bags made of scrap materials and filled with beans. Children toss them in the air and perform a juggling act.

Otouchan – Daddy. Young children usually call their fathers by this name.

Otousan – Father. Young children call their fathers "*Otouchan.*" When they grow up, Father is called *Otousan*, a more formal and respectful name.

Oyatsu – Japanese snacks that children look forward to eating after school.

Shiro – A popular name for white dogs in Japan. *Shiro* means white in color.

FIG 02: SHIRO, KEIKO'S DOG

"*Sugoi!*" – "Wow, big beyond imagination!"

Tabi – Traditional Japanese socks. Ankle-high and with a separation between the big toe and other toes. They are worn by men and women with *geta*.
SEE ALSO *Geta*

"*Tadaima!*" – "I'm home!"

"*Tadaima Okaachan*" – "I'm home, Mommy."

Takoyaki – Grilled octopus balls. They are filled with minced octopus and batter and cooked in a special *takoyaki* pan. This popular Japanese snack is often sold by street vendors who roll their carts into the neighborhoods shouting, "*Takoyaki, takoyaki!*"

Tennou-heika – Emperor of Japan

Undoukai – Sport day. These events are staged by many schools in which students take part in competitive sporting activities. Each wear a white or a red band around their heads so the teams can be distinguished as they are performing relay races, tug-of-war, and other sports.

Ureshii – Happy.

"*Wakatta?*" – "Do you understand?"

Yomogi – Wild leaves from the Chrysanthemum family that grow in most parts of Japan. Leaves are used to make Japanese confectionary.

Yukata – A casual and simple kimono made of cotton. These colorful styled garments are worn in the summer months in Japan, while celebrating various festivals.

"*Yuyake- koyake-de-hi-ga-kurete… yama —no-otera-no-kane-ga-na-ru*" – Japanese children's song continues on as, "*O-te-te-tsunaide-minna-kaero,*" meaning, "The mountain temple's bell rings in the light of a beautiful sunset, let's all go home, holding each other's hands."

Zori – Thongs made of straw.

ACKNOWLEDGMENTS

My deepest appreciation and gratitude to those who have walked with me through the two-and-a-half year journey of writing this book. I have made many friends, but most of all, I feel honored to work side by side with people who have supported and pushed me forward to share my story with the world.

Members of the Omoide Writing Group: I admire you for caring enough to share your internment stories so that future generations can learn about an important chapter in our history. Your inspiring stories were the impetus that led me to write about my own experiences depicting life across the ocean during World War II. A special thank you to Atsushi Kiuchi, Dee Goto, Janine Brodein, and Janet Baba for your leadership in keeping the Omoide group alive and thriving.

Nikki Lewis: You pushed me to the point of tears when you helped me to express my deepest feelings, no matter how painful. You honestly told me, "This chapter is weak. Come out with the truth and it will become a fabulous chapter." Thank you, Nikki. You are by far the best coach I could have asked for.

Randy Tada: A special thanks to my genius cousin for the hours you invested in reading , editing, and giving me priceless advice. When my chapters went through your vigorous critique and came out alive at the other end, I knew they were good. How you were able to edit twelve pages of draft writing in twenty minutes, I will never know.

Wendy Tada: My other genius cousin, who is just as special as her brother. I appreciate your reminders. "A seven-year-old doesn't use these words. Think back and say them as you would have when you were a child." You also opened my eyes to a larger vision. This story is about more than my personal life experiences; it is a story that applies to the millions of immigrants, migrants, and refugee children who are living in two worlds today.

Jean Nishi: You had a way of consistently offering me your personal voice of reason. Your comments always made me feel comfortable and secure. You spent hours of time with me, editing and correcting my sentence structures and thought processes. Thank you for your positive reinforcement and being my good friend.

Special clients of Studio 904: Betsy Diffendal, Beverly Hosea, Valerie Cochran, Tamara Turner, Susan Acker, Barbara Eckert, Peggy

Orem, and many more, thank you for your encouraging words. Every time you came to Studio 904, you'd ask, "How is your book coming along? I can hardly wait to read it." I appreciate your gentle pushes when I felt like I wanted to give up.

Elaine Ikoma Ko: Thank you for introducing me to Chin Music Press. You generously gave up your personal time to guide me through the complex process of book publishing. You were always available, ready to help when I needed your advice. I admire you for your steadfast belief in helping your sisters.

Elaine and Eric Tanaka: Thank you for stepping up to say, "We would like to become financial investors in your book project." Your only reason was "because this story should be shared to inspire others in this world." I appreciate your kind gesture and am grateful for your generosity.

Studio 904's team: When I founded this business thirty-eight years ago, I never dreamed I would have the privilege of working with a team that I enjoy so much. Thank you for allowing me the time and the freedom of mind to write and bring this book to its conclusion. It is because of you that I love coming to work every day. A special thank you to Kaoru Nukui who advised me on the correct usage of the Japanese words in this book.

My husband Tom and special kids, Ross, Linda, and Sheri: I have the best family in the world. Your continued love and support over the years has given me the courage to write and share the story of your courageous grandmother, Mary Fujiye. She taught me so much, but I've learned equally as much from being a wife and mother to you.

Steve Okawa: You are the ultimate designer and a good friend. I am certain that developing an original design concept with another headstrong artist was not an easy task for you — especially when I didn't have any of the answers to your probing questions like "What do you want? What's your vision?" I promise that I will have more clarity as I mature as a writer.

Bruce Rutledge and Chin Music Press: Last, but not least, my heartfelt thanks to Bruce Rutledge and his staff. I was so happy when you saw the potential in my story and equally as excited when you wrote to tell me, "Yes, we will take this project on." You have allowed me the freedom to express my creativity in every page of my book. Thank you for preserving the work of good writers.